OXFORD MEDICAL PUBLICATIONS

Ageing

ALSO PUBLISHED BY OXFORD UNIVERSITY PRESS

Ageing

THE FACTS
SECOND EDITION

NICHOLAS CONI

*Consultant Physician in Geriatric Medicine,
Addenbrooke's Hospital and
Associate Lecturer in the Faculty of
Clinical Medicine, University of Cambridge
Cambridge, UK*

WILLIAM DAVISON

*Emeritus Consultant Physician in Geriatric Medicine
Addenbrooke's Hospital
Cambridge, UK*

STEPHEN WEBSTER

*Consultant Physician in Geriatric Medicine,
Addenbrooke's Hospital and
Associate Lecturer in the Faculty of
Clinical Medicine, University of Cambridge
Cambridge, UK*

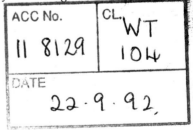
OXFORD   NEW YORK   TOKYO
OXFORD UNIVERSITY PRESS
1992

Oxford University Press, Walton Street, Oxford OX2 6DP
Oxford New York Toronto
Delhi Bombay Calcutta Madras Karachi
Petaling Jaya Singapore Hong Kong Tokyo
Nairobi Dar es Salaam Cape Town
Melbourne Auckland
and associated companies in
Berlin Ibadan

Oxford is a trade mark of Oxford University Press

Published in the United States
by Oxford University Press, New York

First edition published 1984

A catalogue record for this book is available from the British Library
Data available

Library of Congress Cataloging in Publication Data
Coni, Nicholas.
Aging : the facts / Nicholas Coni, William Davison, Stephen
Webster.—2nd ed.
(Oxford medical publications)
Includes bibliographica references and index.
1. Aged—Diseases. 2. Aging. 3. Gerontology. I. Davison,
William, Dr. II. Webster, Stephen. III. Title. IV. Series.
[DNLM: 1. Aged. 2. Aging. WT 104 C751a]
RC952.5.C65 1992 91–398486
ISBN 0–19–262149–1 (pbk.)
ISBN 0–19–262150–5 (hbk.)

Typeset by Cambridge Composing (UK) Ltd
Printed in Great Britain by
Biddles Ltd, Guildford & King's Lynn

Preface to the second edition

During the eight years which have elapsed since the first edition of this book was published, there has been a massive growth in the literature on ageing. The increasing interest in the subject reflects its growing importance on both the economic and sociological scenes throughout the world. It would be gratifying to report that the lot of older people had improved during this period, or that attitudes were better informed, but there is little reason to suppose that this is universally the case. Nevertheless, medical science has advanced and political changes have occurred and we have new information and ideas to impart. We hope that this book will serve both as a description of the various aspects of ageing and as a manual to guide our readers through the many challenges posed by their own ageing or that of their close relatives.

Cambridge N.C.
April 1992 W.D.
  S.W.

Contents

1 The world grows grey   1
2 The benefits of an ageing society   12
3 Retirement—the opportunity of age   19
4 Living arrangements   27
5 Physical disability   35
6 Servicing an ageing society   41
7 The biology of ageing   48
8 'Normal' ageing   54
9 The body's chemical and physical composition   63
10 The ageing brain   71
11 Age-related psychological problems   80
12 Stroke, Parkinson's disease, and motor neurone disease   90
13 Mobility   97
14 Nutrition and digestion   112
15 The bladder and its control   124
16 Heart, blood vessels, and lungs   129
17 Eyes, ears, teeth, skin, and feet   136
18 Cancer   148
19 Medicines   158
20 Caring for an infirm elderly person at home   167
21 Death   176
22 Bereavement   187
Further reading   194
Appendix A: Glossary   195
Appendix B: Useful addresses   200
Index   203

1 The world grows grey

Almost 600 years elapsed between the Black Death and the end of the Second World War, but despite these and other intervening local difficulties of varying magnitudes of horror there was never any special reason to doubt that the future of mankind itself was assured. The principal preoccupation was which of the currently warring factions would emerge victorious. But now the world has grown up, and man has learned that his very survival as a species is threatened. We have become accustomed to living under the merging shadows of the nuclear holocaust, the depletion of the earth's resources, the desecration of the environment, and the population explosion. But among the shadows many gleams of light can be discerned and it is the intention of this book to bring into focus one which brightens the last of these shadows. The growth in the world's population is indeed disastrous, but within the overall growth there are shifts of emphasis resulting in an increase in the proportion of elderly people. It seems to be a good time to be born, because the chances of surviving into advanced age are growing better and better. It is this change and the challenges it poses both to society and to the individual, that we shall be considering.

It has been suggested that at least a quarter, and possibly a third, of all those human beings who have ever lived beyond the age of 60 are alive today. The study of demography is now sufficiently advanced that estimates relating to the past are very much less reliable than those which relate to the future, since in many countries adequate statistics have only become available during the post-war era. The trends, nevertheless, are clear. In the developed world, and increasingly in many parts of the developing world, once a person is born he, and especially she, is likely to enjoy a long life. This characteristic as applied to a society is known as senescence and is a new phenomenon. Earlier human populations, and wild animal populations, do not show senescence. Their numbers show a continuous and almost random attrition from birth onwards throughout life, so that few individuals survive to grow old. Most people would probably look upon senescence as an inherently desirable feature of society, although they might not necessarily regard their own personal senescence, or ageing, quite so favourably.

Nature does not behave in a mathematically perfect pattern, and it remains true even in affluent societies that the new-born baby is more vulnerable than the adult, and that a few seriously impaired babies continue to be born and contribute to the infant mortality statistics. Equally, we will never eliminate premature loss of life due to the toll exacted by the motor car and by major disasters. In addition people, especially young men and women, will always experiment with high-risk activities which may be admirable (mountaineering, hang-gliding) or of an antisocial nature (substance abuse, promiscuity).

Similarly, the attrition throughout life which has been mentioned in connection with other species and other ages is never entirely random. The blackbirds on the lawn face death by starvation and freezing during harsh winters, but their chicks face greater dangers from domestic cats and other predators. When Neanderthal man was sent out of the cave by Neanderthal woman with instructions not to return without some spare triceratops ribs for Sunday lunch, he was liable to be gored through by the five metre tusk of a passing rogue mammoth. But if he was in his prime he might just have escaped by climbing a nearby tree, whereas Neanderthal pensioner would have found such a feat beyond his capabilities. So although primitive man, like wild animals, was from the moment of his birth subject to the random depredations of disease, trauma, famine, and carnivores, there was not a constant rate of attrition of a given population group (cohort). A better model of random attrition is provided by the fate of a batch of glass tumblers purchased by a cafeteria, which are thereafter haphazardly destroyed by customers and washing-up staff until none remain, although even canteen glasses, if badly chipped, become more prone to breakage. The probability of death in any given day, week, or year for an individual human being, on the other hand, increases with age, and doubles every eight years after the age of 30. Individual senescence in man can therefore be seen as an increasing risk of death. Human mortality seems to be at its lowest at the age of 12.

The fate of a group of individuals can best be demonstrated graphically by means of a survival curve. The survival curves of some human populations are shown in Fig 1.1. This shows how the

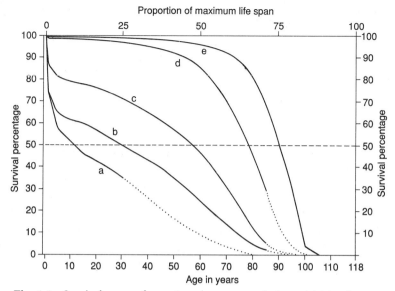

Fig. 1.1 Survival curves for various human populations; (a) Manchester, England, early 1840s; (b) USA, non-white men, 1900–02; (c) USA, white males, 1900–02; (d) USA, total population, 1982; (e) hypothetical western population with minimum disorders.

Source: Warnes, A. (1989). In *Human ageing and later life*, (ed. A. M. Warnes). Edward Arnold, London.

progressive elimination of infantile, childhood, and premature adult mortality has progressively altered the human survival curve in developed nations to produce the appearance known as 'rectangularization'. In such nations, mankind has in recent years become the first and only species to rejoice in the happy expectation of entering the world with an excellent chance of surviving until the end of his natural life. Mortality rates are steadily decreasing during infancy, childhood, adolescence, and adulthood, but they increase steeply in old age.

The shape of the population

Projected figures for future trends in the age structure of the population give the overwhelming impression that the picture differs considerably from one part of the world to another (Table 1.1). The mature societies are represented by the European nations,

Table 1.1   Projected future population.

Region	Population 1985 (millions)	Projected population 2025 (millions)	% aged 65+ 1985	% aged 65+ 2025	% aged 75+ 1985–6
Europe	492	524	12.4	18.4	
Americas	668	1124	7.3	11.1	
Africa	555	1620	3.0	3.9	
Asia	2818	4535	4.7	10.0	
World	4840	8210	5.9	9.7	
UK	56*	56	15.1*	18.7	6.4
USA	246.3	311.9	11.7	17.2	4.9
China	1110.9	1475.1	5.3	12.9	1.3†
France	55.3	58.4	12.4	19.3	6.4
Japan	123.3	132.1	10.0	20.3	

* 1989
† 1982

Source: *World populations prospects* (1986). United Nations, New York.

where there is a low rate of population growth, a low birth-rate, a hitherto steep rise in the numbers of older people during the present century but a levelling out with a shift within the retired population towards a much greater proportion of 'old old' (75- or 80-plus) rather than 'young old' (65-plus) during the latter years of the century. There are worries about the size of the future work-force and its capacity to fulfil the labour-intensive and generally poorly remunerated task of supporting the frail and aged members of society.

The other side of the coin is seen among the developing nations, whose population is continuing to climb. The birth-rate remains high (bad) but infant and childhood mortality is falling (good), so improved survival ensures rising numbers of people living into their late 60s and beyond. Numbers of 'old old' are yet to soar dramatically. The main anxieties about this scenario are centred around the intergenerational friction that old members of these societies will face in competing with the expanding numbers of younger people for the very limited resources available. The nations of the New World (such as the USA and Australia) are experiencing continued population expansion due largely to immigration which swells the young age-groups, and at the same time a shift among the older sections of the populace towards more advanced ages so there will be greater numbers of persons of advanced age. There remain exceptional countries like China whose massive experiment in demographic regulation (one child per family) is likely to lead to unforeseen consequences, depending on the degree of the compliance of the Chinese people.

Why do populations age?

It is a common misconception that the credit—or the blame—for the rising tide of older people can be laid at the door of the medical profession. In point of fact, so-called curative medicine makes

Table 1.2 Expectation of further years of life (UK) at different ages (figures in brackets are expected years in 1891).

At age	Men	Women
0	71.5 (41.9)	77.4 (45.7)
5	67.5	73.2
10	62.5	68.2
15	57.6	63.3
20	52.8	58.4
25	48.0	53.5
30	43.2	48.6
35	38.4	43.7
40	33.7	38.9
45	29.0	34.2
50	24.6 (17.5)	29.6 (19.3)
55	20.4	25.2
60	16.6 (11.9)	21.0 (13.0)
65	13.2 (9.5)	17.2 (10.4)
70	10.3 (7.3)	13.6 (8.0)
75	7.9 (5.6)	10.4 (6.1)
80	5.9 (3.9)	7.6 (4.3)
85	4.4	5.4

Source: Government Actuary's Department (1988). *Annual abstract of statistics* (Table 2.23). HMSO, London

extremely little impact upon the longevity of a population. The incidence of tuberculosis in the United Kingdom, for example, was rapidly declining long before the advent of effective chemotherapy. Despite modern drugs and surgical techniques, the expectation of life of a 65-year-old Englishman was only just over 3.5 years longer in 1982–3 than it had been 90 years previously (Table 1.2). His wife, it is true, had fared somewhat better, and the figures in the USA are comparable at age 60—a further 22 years for a woman, a further 17 for a man. This is in contrast to the dramatic transformation in the life expectancy at birth which occurred between those dates.

There are two main factors which influence the age structure of a population—its fertility, or birth-rate, and its infant and childhood mortality.

Birth rate

To state the obvious, the more live births per female, the higher the proportion of young people in the community. Birth-rates fluctuate a great deal over the years. The end of the seventeenth century was a period of fertility in Great Britain, and as a consequence, early in the eighteenth century more than ten per cent of the population was aged over 60, a figure which then declined to 6.5 or 7 per cent and remained there until the present century. There was a marked decline in fertility in this country after about 1870, and a further fall during the first third of this century. Fertility rates have dropped again in European countries since 1964–65. The French have calculated that each woman needs to bear 2.2 children simply to replace the generations, but with characteristic capriciousness each Frenchwoman is currently only producing 1.96 babies. The birth-rate in that country fell from about 17 per 1000 inhabitants in 1971 to 14 in 1978: the birth rate in the USA in 1980 was 15 per 1000. By way of contrast, a number of the developing nations have birth-rates over 40 per 1000 (for example Bangladesh, Pakistan, and Paraguay) which is sufficient to double their numbers in 35 or 40 years. The birth-rate in Kenya is 53 per 1000. These countries are all likely to continue to have a demographic structure heavily dominated by the young.

Decrease in child and infant mortality

Whatever one's view about the desirability of a falling birth-rate, the second factor which leads to a relative growth in the proportion of elderly people in the population is an unmitigated blessing. It is the enormous reduction in infant and childhood mortality in the UK and other developed nations over the past 75 years or so. This is mainly a result of the virtual elimination of the infectious diseases as a cause of death—an advance which owes more to improved standards of housing, heating, nutrition, and sanitation, than to medical treatment. At the end of the eighteenth century, 50 out of 100 children died before their tenth birthdays and only six lived to be 60. As recently as the First World War, the infant mortality rate in the UK claimed more lives than the carnage of the trenches. In the affluent countries, this situation has completely changed, so that sickness and death are increasingly the preserves of older people—the tricks that fate keeps up her sleeve until you reach the age of 60 or 65. However, this happy state of affairs is far from universal, and throughout the world, millions of people are exposed to conditions such as malaria, bilharzia, malnutrition, and AIDS which show scant respect for the vitality of youth. Just 15 years ago it was true that in Africa, Asia, and Latin America, half of all deaths occurred in children under five. In most parts of these continents, this appalling toll has since then been drastically reduced.

Is the human lifespan increasing?

The lifespan of a species is the age at which the average individual would die if there were no premature loss of life through disease or accidents. In the case of man, this might be 85 or even 90 years. The survival curves shown in Fig. 1.1 are all depicted terminating between 80 and 105, suggesting that almost 100 per cent of the population would have died by this age. Indeed, it is necessary, if the survival curve is to achieve the rectangular shape we spoke of, that all curves should finish at the same point. This has led some authors to envisage a rosy scenario whereby avoidable illness is indeed increasingly avoided, thereby relieving society of the burden of chronic dependency caused by strokes, coronary artery disease, chronic bronchitis, and cancer of the lung, to quote four examples. We will thus enjoy good health until we attain our lifespan, when we will die following a mercifully brief final illness.

But this is not the whole story. As we have seen, the life

expectancies of older age-groups have not increased as dramatically
during the past century as have those at birth, but the increases in
the UK do continue to be significant nevertheless. At age 85, life
expectancy rose by 6 months (to 4.6 years for men and 5.6 years
for women) between 1970–72 and 1978–80). Properly authenticated
longevity records are regularly broken (the current record is over
120 years and is held by a Japanese man), although there is an
element of inevitability about this. By analogy with athletics, all
records must eventually be broken, especially as now there are so
many more people living and so many of them are fitter. In the UK
the Queen sends her congratulations to each of her subjects who
celebrates his or her 100th birthday. In 1951 271 of these messages
were sent; in 1981, the Queen sent 2410.

Perhaps it is encouraging to reflect that man appears to be the
longest lived mammal. Humans also live longer than the birds, for
despite unconfirmed claims of vastly ancient cockatoos and vul-
tures, none has been shown to live much longer than 80 years.
Some fish may be capable of living for well over a century, and the
Carolina box-tortoise has been recorded as living for 129 years (see
Table 7.1, on p. 52).

If we are living longer, is it a good thing?

The answer is, it all depends. If we are simply fulfilling our rightful
lifespan and remaining fitter until the end, that must be good. If we
are adding extra years to that lifespan, and those years are years of
dependency and incapacity, few would welcome such an addition.
Unfortunately, there is some evidence that the latter is a truer
picture of events than the former. A study of the records of over
24 000 admissions to long-term geriatric hospital care over a period
of 32 years in Belfast revealed, encouragingly, that the average age
on admission rose steadily throughout this period, suggesting a rise
in active life expectancy. Less encouraging was the finding that the
length of hospital stay increased, and still less, the rise in the
proportion of the total lifespan spent in long-term care. This
suggests that the more people in their 90s there are, the more
invalids there are, and this has been called 'the failure of our
success'.

Eric Midwinter, formerly Director of the Centre for Policy on
Ageing, recently defined the four ages of man. The first is 'child-

hood and social apprenticeship; the second age of work and parenting; the third age of the independent pinnacles of life beyond paid work and raising a family; the fourth age that of dependence and ultimately, death.' He champions the cause of a 'long, happy and glorious third age, with the fourth age put off for as lengthy a time as possible and then itself being brief, merciful and painless.' Few would disagree.

Our chances of enjoying a third age

Peter Laslett, the social historian and director of the Rank Xerox Unit on Ageing at Cambridge, has tried to quantify the chance of someone who has reached the age of 25, which he arbitrarily takes as the start of the second age, reaching 70, which he regards as a point in our life when we might have enjoyed some years in the third age in the company of others. This chance is fairly readily calculated by dividing the number of persons surviving to the age of 70 by the number surviving to 25. He calls this figure the third age indicator, and in the UK in 1981–83 it was 0.779 for women and 0.634 for men. In 1901, it was 0.456 for women and 0.375 for men. It was not until 1950 that a figure of 0.5 was surpassed by males in France, the USA, and the UK, although their counterparts in New Zealand had done so in 1901 and countries such as Mexico and Japan were only some ten years behind. The third age is here to stay as an important part of our lives, and the sooner society and the individual takes cognizance of the fact the better.

The British scene

The British population structure has shifted towards a much less youth-dominated and more even distribution of age-groups during the twentieth century. Figure 1.2 brings out the current expansion in the over-75 age-range in bar-chart form. Table 1.3 gives statistics concerning the over-80s, as well as for the 65–79-year-olds, and enumerates the predicted growth until the year 2023.

The global perspective

Numbers of older people are set to rise in the developing nations as well as in the western world, and birth-rates are likely to decline to a variable and rather unpredictable extent. The predicted world

Ageing: the facts

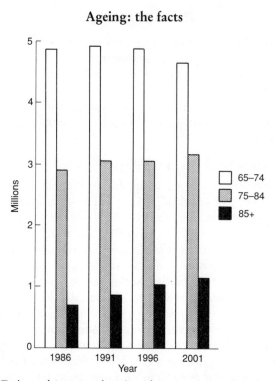

Fig. 1.2   Estimated (1986) and projected (1991, 1996, and 2001) population of Great Britain by age, 1989.

Source (estimate for 1986): OPCS (1991). *Population trends*, **66**. HMSO, London.
Source (projections for 1991, 1996, and 2001): OPCS (1991). *National population projections 1989-based*, Series PP2, No. 17. HMSO, London.

Table 1.3 Projected population growth (UK) in thousands

	THOUSANDS U.K.					
	1989	*1993*	*1998*	*2003*	*2013*	*2023*
65–79	6852	6747	6681	6421	7104	7918
80+	1989	2139	2141	2322	2391	2550

Projections—O.P.C.S.   Based 1983
(Central Statistical Office 1987)

	USA figures for comparison			
	1989	*2000*	*2020*	*2023*
All 65+	27 831	35 480	52 026	53 708
85+		4534	6424	

population pyramid will begin to assume the European shape, but the European nations are on the whole anticipating a smaller increase in their elderly populations than are the Asian and American peoples. The equitable allocation of resources to support the more dependent citizens of some of these countries is likely to be a major political and economic challenge.

2   The benefits of an ageing society

Ageing as a personal benefit

Age adds depth and breadth to life. It is a privilege and opportunity to have the good fortune to live and to lead a long and active life. The extra time allows the development of new skills and the perfection of talents. Longevity also allows you to enjoy and share the lives of many generations, both those ahead of you and those behind—perhaps as many as six generations in all—a span of 150 or more years!

The responsibilities of aged people

The 15 per cent or so of our society that elderly people make up is too large a proportion to be ignored or wasted. It is also too large a group to be encouraged to live a parasitic existence. The skills and talents of this group, as outlined elsewhere in this chapter, are too valuable and too scarce to be allowed to go to waste.

How to avoid being a burden

Keep yourself fit

This not only means adopting regular physical and mental activity as recommended in the next chapter; it also means that you should attempt to adopt the healthy lifestyle that you always knew you should. Improve your diet (see Chapter 14) by eating more fresh fruit and vegetables but less fat and refined sugars. Keep your alcohol intake in check and give up smoking, if you haven't already. It is never too late to take up good habits, and even in very late life such improvements in life-style can pay practical dividends in improving the general feeling of well-being. Always remember that your health is your own responsibility.

Do not take unnecessary risks

It has to be accepted that life becomes more dangerous with increasing age. However, a careful assessment needs to be made between risks and benefits from any activity—whether for pleasure or necessity. Do not tempt danger by having an unsafe house. Do not drive if you are no longer capable of doing so safely (Chapter 13). Do listen to advice—especially about dangerous substances, such as medications (Chapter 19) and alcohol.

Consider the feelings and anxieties of others

Fierce independence can earn great admiration but may also precipitate reasonable fear and anxiety in others. Those that love and cherish you may not be as mentally strong as you are, and may therefore find it increasingly difficult to accept your determination to remain independent at all costs. Recognize their fears and the honest and good reasons for them. Be prepared to compromise on some issues if only for the sake of others.

Do not use your age as a weapon

You would rightly be offended to have your age given as an excuse for shoddy treatment, for example by your doctor ('What do you expect at your age, my dear?'). In return for proper respect you must not expect others to give way to you just because of your age. You must continue to argue your case, in whatever matter, with logic and reason and not practise emotional blackmail.

How to be an ageing asset

Society owes much to its aged members, for their achievements, their hard work, taxes, and their love and care in years past. However, the role of aged people is not one of passivity and retrospect, and the elderly are not just our living history. They are also part of our present and our future.

Become a volunteer

The traditional pool of volunteer labour is shrinking as more middle-aged, middle-class women take paid employment and young women fail to give up employment on becoming mothers. The gap left can only be filled by adolescents and elderly people.

The latter bring wide experience and can offer continuity for ten or more years. Many services now depend almost entirely on elderly volunteers, for example, the meals on wheels service, the hospital car service, the guides and custodians in museums and National Trust properties, and the Leagues of Friends of Hospitals and other institutions. By becoming involved in such activities you can not only provide a valuable community service, but you will also find the opportunity of developing new interests and of broadening your own horizons.

Become an adviser

In a rapidly changing society the knowledge of machines and techniques has a short shelf-life and rapidly becomes outdated. Fortunately human behaviour changes less rapidly and perhaps not at all. Skills acquired during a long life with regard to counselling and advising remain valuable. It is the elderly who have these talents, which can be indispensable in organizations, such as the Citizens' Advice Bureau, CRUSE, the Samaritans, and many other support groups.

Become a carer

This usually happens more by accident than by choice. However most carers are pensioners. Most do a magnificent job and with great dedication. It is an important role which should be taken seriously by society in general and carers in particular. More help and support is needed to sustain carers. The more carers there are the easier the task will become and the better the recognition of their role. Caring need not be only for other elderly people as carers are also needed for children (grandchildren) and youger, disabled people. The range of need is wide and the opportunities therefore great.

Become a 'teacher'

The elderly have much to teach other age groups. Commonly, the greater the age difference between pupil and teacher, the greater the satisfaction to both participants. The great natural affinity that often occurs between children and their grandparents is evidence of this mutual appreciation. Socrates was 70 years old when he was accused of corrupting the young with his teachings. It was perhaps his success and popularity, as much as the content, which particularly threatened the security of his political rulers.

As the value and interest of oral history are increasingly appreciated, there should be more and more opportunities for the elderly to share their earlier experiences. Thus the young can be taught a richer and fuller understanding of our society's past. Contemporary and live commentaries of historic events recorded on film greatly enhance the experience of the viewers, especially when they are young and impressionable. The technique can be used nationally (on television), locally in schools, and amongst friends, neighbours, and family. Opportunities are therefore open to most elderly people with a desire to recount and describe their previous experiences—but be discreet.

Many politicians continue to teach us about our past when they reminisce after retirement, on television interviews, in newspaper articles and guest lectures, or in their autobiographies. Harold MacMillan—born in 1894—became a favourite political commentator, even of his previous political opponents, his accounts and interpretation of twentieth-century history being valued by all.

Dame Freya Stark, even in her nineties, was still travelling widely and was able from her own experience to teach us of the changes which have occurred in the Middle East during the past 50 years. Pablo Casals, (1876–1973) was conducting and teaching the cello until his 80th birthday. Famous dancers, such as Ninettte de Vallois, have been able to offer encouragement and opportunity to the young, and although no longer able to practise their art, they have been instrumental in setting up schools and performing companies.

Clearly the elderly have much to offer. We must not hesitate to use them. We must not be too proud to learn from their previous experiences, including their mistakes. The older the person, the more precious is his knowledge as much of it will die with him if not collected and preserved.

Examples of successful ageing

Elderly people in public life

In public and political life we find the most impressive examples of elderly people being successful in the management of their fellows. Opinions as to whether this is a creditable achievement or otherwise depends on one's own philosophy. For example, Ronald Reagan was born in 1911 and after a variety of careers became president of the USA, the most powerful democratic block in the world's history. His counterparts in the USSR, until recently, have nearly all been of similar seniority.

Winston Churchill (1874–1965), after a long period in politics (which included several changes of party), became wartime Prime Minister at the time in life when most people face compulsory retirement. His most active and influential years were between his 65th and 80th birthdays. He died (aged 90) ten years after his resignation from the post of Prime Minister. It is also worth noting that our recent Prime Minister, Mrs Margaret Thatcher, has now for several years been eligible for a state pension. Mr Edward Heath, a previous UK Prime Minister, at the age of 74 was invited to the Middle East during the 1991 Gulf crisis as a special envoy to negotiate the return of ill and aged Gulf war hostages (the majority younger than Mr Heath himself).

At the time of writing Her Majesty, Queen Elizabeth, the Queen Mother, at over 90 years of age remains active and involved in contemporary life. Her example provides many people with inspiration and admiration and clearly illustrates the special contribution that elderly people can make to enrich society in general.

Lord Soper, when well into his 80s, continued to lead an active public life. He continued to speak regularly at Hyde Park Corner and Tower Hill, and just after his 80th birthday took part in a patriotism debate in the Oxford Union to mark the famous 1933 debate on King and Country. Lord Soper was supporting the argument for unilateral disarmament, a movement he had supported since its start in the 1950s.

Lord Bertram Russell (1872–1970) was another person who, in the minds of many people, was best associated with the peace movement in his old age. However his skills were much wider, ranging from mathematician to writer and philosopher. He lived to be 98 and even in his final year he remained strongly convinced by the unilateralist argument and actively supported the movement.

Lord Denning retired as Master of the Rolls in 1982 when he was aged 83. He was famous (or infamous) for his decisions. After retirement he remained in the limelight and aired his views publicly as ever.

Clearly all these examples have been or are exceptional people. Their views and objectives vary enormously. Their common denominator is that they have all acquired skills in influencing, persuading, and managing other people. Their success is partly due to opportunities to polish and perfect ability through long and active lives. They have also been fortunate enough to remain fit and active, even in very old age, and have thus been able to continue to make valuable contributions to our society. In our own modest ways some opportunities are open to all of us.

Elderly people in the arts

Old age is the final phase of growth and development. The longer we live, the greater will have been the opportunities to achieve the fullest possible progress. To live into old age therefore gives the greatest chance of fulfilment of potential. Ageing usually implies a deterioration but we should not assume that this is universal to all human activities and talents.

Some talents are transient and fail to deliver the final promise or fruits. Usually such failure reflects a passing fashion which proves to be fleeting, although a retrospective view may negate such opinions. However, many artists, writers, and preformers practise and develop their skills throughout a long and productive life. Progression of techniques and ideas then provide inspiration and guidance to others. What works would Van Gogh have produced had he lived beyond his 37 years, or Keats, if he had not died at 26? Suppose Jane Austen had lived longer than 42 years or Mozart survived beyond his 35 years? It is an interesting academic exercise to consider these possibilities. Fortunately many examples of productive longevity are available and we are able to benefit from work produced at the end of successful careers. Examples are most easily found amongst the arts, but lifelong development can also be observed in other fields. Picasso (1881–1973) led such a long and productive life that it provides us with one of the best examples of progression in work and technique. As an adolescent he painted in the style of the old masters. At the beginning of the twentieth century he produced his blue period, then moved on to the pink period. He experimented with cubism and moved into surrealism and expressionism as violence swept across Europe. After the Second World War more gentle themes and methods returned. His work thus illustrates not only his own development but also that of his environment. Even after his death he continued to make his mark, as when his painting of Guernica, painted in 1937, was returned to Spain when democracy was established there.

The Cinema is very much a product of this century. Some of its earlier pioneers were able to grow with its development. Charlie Chaplin is a universally known example. Having started in English music hall, he was able to adapt to silent film comedy, introducing social comment and characterization within his slapstick films made during the years of the First World War. Although somewhat reluctant to make the transition to sound films he did successfully move on in the 1930s and continued to make films until his old age in the 1960s. He was deeply involved in the commercial aspects of film-making as well as taking starring roles. 1990 produced a further example in the film industry of success in the late stages of a long career. Jessica Tandy was awarded the Oscar for the best actress in the film 'Driving Miss Daisy'. At the time of the award she was over 80.

An advantage of advanced age is a healthy disrespect for previous constraints. Arthur Rubenstein lived to 95 and played in concerts throughout his 80s. At the end of his career he enjoyed increased freedom as he no longer felt restricted by the opinions of critics and others and had reached a position of financial security which led to new adventures in music.

3 Retirement—the opportunity of age

It is no longer acceptable to think of the period of retirement as the twilight years. It is true that most people make some sacrifices when they retire from paid employment. Income is likely to be reduced—but occupational pensions are becoming more common and offer greater financial security. Status may change, especially for those who have become over-dependent on the trappings associated with their employment. The camaraderie of the workplace will also be missed.

In contrast to these losses there are potentially many gains. Retirement should be looked upon as a period of opportunity. It is after all a period which may last for more than 30 years—why should you not find as much to enjoy in the third age as in the first and second, even if your aims and priorities are rather different.

Planning before retirement

This cannot start too soon—in fact we should all be planning our retirement throughout our lives. Even schoolchildren should receive instruction about retirement. Such information would enable the young to have a better understanding of ageing and some insight into the complexities of being old. Young people should also be given the time and opportunity to experiment with interests, hobbies, and leisure pursuits. Such recreational activities may have no immediate relevance to their future employment, but may introduce them to activities which give pleasure and enjoyment. Having dabbled with an interest in your youth, you may have to wait until old age affords another opportunity for it to be developed and enjoyed to the full. Therefore, as retirement approaches it is important to consider what interests and activities you have previously enjoyed and can now revert to.

Financial planning must also start early. For a secure retirement a nest-egg (capital) is desirable and adequate revenue (income) must be assured. State benefits are likely to be at subsistence level only and additional pension arrangements should be made, either through your employment or individually. Attention will need to be paid to the unfortunate fact that most married women will spend some of their lives as widows. Wills should be drawn up and reviewed in the light of changing circumstances. This is especially important if family relationships have become strained or complicated. Remarriage may bring additional complications. Your living accommodation must be prepared during your working life—so that large and unexpected expenditure can be avoided during retirement, unless the decision is taken to relocate. (Chapter 4).

When and how to retire

Until recently there were increasing pressures to persuade people to retire early. This was a consequence of high unemployment in the UK and other parts of the western world. However, for the remainder of this century and for the beginning of the next, the situation will be remarkably different, except during recessions. Demographic changes will result in a fall in the number of young people entering the employment market. To compensate, older people will be encouraged to remain at work or even to retrain for alternative employment.

The age of retirement is clearly a moveable milestone in life. The fact that the end-points are artificial can be seen from the varying ages used. For example, in the UK, 65 is usual for most men and 60 for women—see Table 3.1 for other examples. In general, people

Table 3.1 Recognized retirement ages (National Provident Institution, based on UK Inland Revenue Practice No. 1990)

Age 35	Athletes, badminton players, dancers, footballers, wrestlers
Age 40	Cricketers, divers, trapeze artists
Age 45	Flat-race jockeys, Royal Marine Reservists
Age 50	Croupiers, martial arts instructors, ITV newscasters, rugby league referees
Age 55	Air pilots, part-time firemen, inshore fishermen, psychiatrists

will be encouraged or persuaded to leave the workforce according to the rules of supply and demand. It is, however, not unreasonable that those whose finances and health are secure should be able to decide for themselves when they wish to make such a major change in their lives.

Those who retire early by choice tend to have happier and longer retirements. Those who have enjoyed variety in life are more likely to do so in retirement than those who have not. A full, broad, and prolonged education is also likely to stand a person in good stead when retirement is reached. Those who have found happiness and fulfilment in work are just as likely to find the same satisfaction in an active retirement.

Retirement is likely to be unhappy when it occurs without warning, choice, or planning—for example, enforced early retirement, due either to redundancy or ill-health. It is the victims of these traumas who are likely to fall as early casualties to death when they cease to work.

If one has complete freedom of choice about the timing of retirement, the next decision is the speed at which the change should be made. For most people withdrawal is sudden, but it need not be so. For some the opportunity to wean themselves off work is an attractive possibility. By working part-time it will be possible to gradually give up responsibilities whilst developing important new activities. A gradual transition from work to retirement will also help to ease the financial changes that are likely to occur. Marital adjustments may also be easier if stopping work is gradual, the shrewd female definition of retirement—'twice as much husband on half as much money'—may be softened by the combination of half-time work and half-time play plus half-time pay.

Enjoying and organizing retirement

Attitudes

If retirement is approached in a happy and enthusiastic way, then it is likely to live up to expectations. Beware of negative attitudes and stereotyping associated with age. Wounding phrases such as 'mutton dressed up as lamb' and 'you can't teach old dogs new tricks' are ready made for putting down those old people who have aspirations.

It would be foolish for older people to compete with youthful persons in the beauty stakes. However, retired people can and should remain attractive and smart—but you will need to use different techniques to those employed in earlier life. The problems will be different and so will the answers, but the obstacles are not insurmountable. If treated properly mutton can be delicious although different to lamb.

Old dogs *can* learn new tricks. This has been clearly demonstrated when classes of old and young pupils have been compared when using identical course material and examinations. In fact, the older learners usually do better because of their higher levels of motivation and their increased self-knowledge which has taught them how to absorb new information more effectively.

Everybody has to find their own way through old age. There are no ready-made role models. It would be wrong to follow slavishly the example of previous generations. The lives of each generation are now so different it would be unrealistic to expect each to result in the same product. Each generation must decide for itself what is right and proper in regard to behaviour. The rules set down by our parents or great-grandparents may well be inappropriate and have to be modified to fit current circumstances. If you, at your age, feel happy and comfortable doing it, then it is right for you. It is important to become bolder with increasing age—just as you will have to learn to tolerate the behaviour, appearances, and activities of the young, so will they have to show tolerance to your preferences.

Social relationships

Increased proximity to your partner may not lead to greater emotional closeness. Retirement may either increase or decrease stresses within the partnership. With the exception of holiday times, it may be the only time that you will have truly lived together. No longer kept apart by employment or family, you may have difficulties in sharing your life together. It may be necessary to re-negotiate tasks and responsibilities if a new equilibrium is to be achieved.

It is a great asset to be of value to others. This is as true in retirement as at other times. Therefore beware of making your spouse redundant and try to remain useful to other members of your family, and to friends and neighbours. This should help you to retain a wide circle of contacts with people of all ages. Try not to retreat into a geriatric ghetto, but do not dissociate yourself from your peers. Comparisons with the latter, especially in regard to physical exertion can help you to judge if you are ageing naturally or pathologically.

Fitness

Fitness is a luxury for the young but an essential for the old! The fitter you are, the less likely you are to become ill and the more likely to make a quick and full recovery should your health break down. It is the elderly who are the most likely to suffer from illness in developed countries—and those illnesses are more likely to be due to degenerative changes in our bodies. Therefore invest in time and effort to become and stay fit as you get older. Pay attention to both physical and mental fitness—to ignore either is to invite disaster.

Physical fitness can be regained and maintained during retirement. Muscles waste due to lack of use during a sedentary life—but they do not disappear and they can be redeveloped (see Chapter 8). How you do this hardly matters—but it is essential that you choose an activity which you enjoy and which gives you pleasure. This self-gratification is important because you will have to persist with your activity on a regular basis—year in and year out. If the activity you choose bores you, you are more likely to give it up. It is not essential to participate in macho and dangerous sports to ensure fitness (but please do so if they appeal to you). Activities such as walking the dog, ballroom-dancing, or cultivating an allotment or garden will all suffice if done regularly and with enthusiasm.

If you are attracted to more vigorous activities, do not be put off by inappropriate attitudes. For example, do not refrain from swimming because you look different in swimming gear to how you looked at 18 years of age. Do not assume that everybody else learned to swim as a child—there are adult classes.

People often assume that taking up exercise in later life will be dangerous. However, that is only the case if you tackle the problem unwisely. Training is needed for any new activity, so start gently and gradually work up to your peak. Whether it takes you weeks, months, or years does not matter so long as you practise regularly and enjoy yourself. Remember that exertion causes even the young to sweat, get breathless, and have palpitations. Only worry if you get these problems earlier or more severely than your contemporaries. Comparisons with the latter are easier if you share exertion with others; for example, in team or group activities. If you are in doubt about your ability to take up or continue a physical activity, then consult your general practitioner.

Mental exercise must not be forgotten—brains may behave like muscles as we grow old, so use it or lose it! You should therefore plan to take up new mental activities in order to develop as well as to maintain your mind. The nature of the subject does not matter—so long as it gives you pleasure. You may wish to learn, re-learn, or improve a foreign language to assist your travel plans or reading. You may join a drama group and participate in amateur productions. You may learn a new subject—just for the hell of it!

There should be no real problems with access to adult education within the UK. If you live centrally in a well-populated area, you should be within easy reach of classes provided by your local education authority, Workers Education Association, University of the Third Age, or other groups and clubs. Even if you live in an isolated area or are restricted in your mobility, you should not be cut off from learning experiences. Distance teaching techniques as developed by the Open University will enable you to participate. The fact that university programmes are screened late at night is not a deterrent as you can always record the programmes on video and view them at a more convenient time.

Always remember that you are never to old to learn. Using your mind may be the best method of keeping it agile and nimble and may offer some protection from dementia.

Health in retirement

Health becomes increasingly vulnerable with increasing age. The combination of progressive degenerative changes, ageing, and reduced resistance to infection, make a breakdown in health more likely. The best tactics to adopt in this battle remain prevention, early detection, early intervention, and active rehabilitation.

Prevention in the form of leading a healthy life-style is a lifelong need. Good habits should be started early and maintained throughout life. Even if your compliance to advice in earlier years has been poor, it is still worthwhile mending your ways in retirement. For example, it is beneficial to give up smoking at any age! Remember, the fitter you are the less likely you are to fall ill.

Early detection and early intervention are closely linked. They depend on having a healthy awareness of your body, noticing any persistent changes, deterioration, or abnormality in function or structure (for example, lumps). You also need to be able to feel free to approach your doctor when you are worried. An enduring relationship with a particular doctor or general practice is a valuable asset. It is essential that you find it easy to relate to your medical adviser and have confidence that your worries and problems will be taken seriously. If you feel a need to change your doctor in later life—and a relocation of your home may make this unavoidable—you should seek out a practitioner with a reputation for empathy with older patients. A doctor who possesses the Diploma in Geriatric Medicine is well qualified to help and advise you. By working for this extra examination he will have indicated his special interest and skills in the health problems of older people.

Active rehabilitation depends mainly on a positive and determined approach to overcome disability. The desire to return to a previously active and enjoyable life acts as a very powerful motivator. Any general fitness you acquire before the onset of illness and disability will help to ensure the best possible recovery. Time and energy invested in fitness and life satisfaction before an illness will pay dividends after a change in health status.

Freedom with discipline

A common reason for the eager anticipation of retirement is the craving to be freed from a rigid routine and timetable inflicted by paid employment. This desire for freedom is understandable but it is also slightly inappropriate. For most people, structure in the life pattern is important and will remain so after retirement. It would be wrong and dangerous to abandon entirely routine and planning. The opportunity provided by retirement is that of restructuring routine. A programme will still be needed but it should be less rigid and less tightly packed. Regular times should still be set aside, but these should now be for more enjoyable and fulfilling activities. For instance, you can establish a time for your physical activities, such as golf or regular walking; some time for learning, for example, your French lesson; time for your voluntary work, for example, meals on wheels; time for your family; and time for yourself. Beware of trying to cram too much into your days—retain the freedom to say no to offers. Remember that your needs and interests may change and develop. Therefore be prepared to review your life and activities from time to time. Do not be afraid to make changes. Use structure and routine to enable you to enjoy your retirement but do not allow yourself to become their slave again.

The negative aspects of retirement

In this chapter we have stressed the positive side of retirement. We have concentrated on the opportunities that retirement offers. However, we must remember the other side of the coin. During retirement you will be faced by unpleasant tasks, situations, and decisions. The dilemmas presenting themselves will not be easy but forethought always helps. Therefore be aware of the potential problems, such as loneliness, bereavement and becoming a carer, and becoming disabled. All of these problems and situations are dealt with in detail later in this book (see Chapters 5, 20, 21, and 22).

4 Living arrangements

Where you live is a major ingredient of your health and happiness. It is therefore right and proper that much time and thought should be devoted to this topic. The decision will not be an easy one and many dilemmas, conflicts of interest, and contradictions will have to be settled. Many personal factors will affect your needs, aspirations, and freedom of choice. All of the following will have to be taken into account:

(1) finance;

(2) family ties and social responsibilities;

(3) preferred life-style;

(4) where to live;

(5) the type of accommodation;

(6) who to live with;

(7) the sort of support will you need and what can you expect (see Chapter 6).

Finance

The greater your affluence the greater your opportunities for choice. However, for most people growing old is associated with a decline in their disposable income (see Tables 4.1 and 4.2). Recently there has been much discussion about WOOPIES (well-off older people) which has attracted the attention of some politicians and the advertising industry. It is true that the distribution of wealth in the United Kingdom is changing. It is reported that 40 per cent of personal wealth in this country is now in the hands of the over 55s. This improvement in the financial position of some elderly people

Table 4.1   National differences in disposable income, inequality, and poverty (from Ageing in Society, Sage Publications)

| | Income, inequality, and poverty according to age | | | | | | | | |
| | Disposable income in relation to national mean[1] | | | Inequality[2] | | | Poverty rates[3] | | |
Country	65–74	75+	All ages	65–74	75+	All ages	65–74	75+	All ages
Canada	0.94	0.81	1.00	0.309	0.291	0.299	11.2	12.1	12.1
W. Germany	0.84	0.77	1.00	0.298	0.340	0.355	12.2	15.2	7.2
Israel	0.92	0.96	1.00	0.360	0.429	0.333	22.6	27.1	14.5
Norway	1.01	0.79	1.00	0.250	0.229	0.243	2.7	7.3	4.8
Sweden	0.96	0.78	1.00	0.143	0.126	0.205	0.0	0.0	5.0
UK	0.76	0.67	1.00	0.266	0.240	0.273	16.2	22.0	8.8
USA	0.99	0.84	1.00	0.342	0.355	0.326	17.8	25.5	16.9
Mean	0.92	0.80	—	0.281	0.287	0.291	11.9	15.6	9.9
SD	0.08	0.08	—	0.067	0.092	0.050	7.5	9.2	4.4

[1] Disposable income (adjusted for family size) as a proportion of the national mean for the total population.
[2] Gini coefficients for distribution of adjusted disposable income within age groups and for total population.
[3] Poverty rate defined as percentage of persons in families with adjusted disposable income below half of the median for all families in the population.

Table 4.2   Sources of income UK, 1984–5.

	Pensioners	Total household income
Wages and salaries	9%	69%
Investment and rent	9%	7%
Private pensions	22%	7%
NI retirement pension	49% ⎱	
Other social security	11% ⎰	16%

is due to a combination in the growth of owner-occupation and the more widespread introduction of occupational pensions.

However, the status of owner-occupiers may be a very mixed blessing. On the positive side, it may provide the owners with the option of trading down. Thus a large family home can be sold to buy a smaller and more suitable dwelling for their declining years, the residue from the transaction being invested to provide regular supplements to income. For other old people the ownership and maintenance of an expensive home may be seen as financially disadvantageous. Emotional ties may discourage them from disposing of their long-term home. Fortunately there are solutions to both dilemmas. The remortgaging of property will allow the participant to reinvest in an annuity and thus provide a regular supplement to income. Clearly, individual circumstances must be taken into account and professional advice and help should be sought. Grants can be claimed to maintain or convert accommodation to make it suitable for new needs. For this purpose, help should be sought from the local authority housing department and voluntary organizations, such as housing associations.

Many elderly people still live in rented accommodation and some rely entirely on state benefits. For these pensioners their period of retirement is going to be one of tight financial arrangements and declining choices.

Family ties and social responsibilities

Responsibilities to family and friends do not disappear at the time of retirement and your role as a giver of care may well persist. Anxieties about the failing health of your parents may dictate that you move nearer to them after your retirement from paid work. The need for child-care (for your grandchildren) may similarly put you under pressure to move nearer to a child and his or her family. Conversely, the need to fulfil these caring roles may prevent you from moving from your long-term residence if your family live nearby and need your help.

Preferred lifestyle

Are you a solitary person or a gregarious one? Are you fiercely independent or happy to rely on others? Do you enjoy country life or city living? These are all very personal decisions but ones which must be made if you are contemplating a move.

Often the personal factors outlined above will dictate the choices that you can make. If that is not the case you should exercise your freedom to choose with great care and introspection.

Where to live

To move or not to move, that is the question. If you are happy in your current accommodation, you must list the assets that you currently enjoy and will not be able to transport. For instance, happy memories are kept fresh in familiar surroundings. Confidence is maintained by familiarity. Good neighbours, upon whom you may need to rely even more in the future, will not move with you.

If any of these factors are essential to your contentment, then stay put. If your accommodation no longer quite fits your needs, then concentrate on improving and adapting what you already have (Table 4.3).

Table 4.3   Where do elderly people live in England?

Age	'At home'	Institutions
Over 65 years	95%	5%
Over 75 years	80%	20%
Over 85 years	75%	25%

When a decision is made to move—try to ensure that the move is for positive reasons. There will also be negative aspects to any move and these should be considered and weighed against the potential benefits.

Do not be trapped by positive factors which are more apparent than real. For instance, being physically nearer to your children may make visiting easier—but it will not provide extra time. Your family may also have to make changes; for example, alter their social or working life to visit you, even if you live nearer. If they are unhappy or unwilling to make such changes, your new proximity will only highlight the reasons why you are not emotionally and socially closer.

Remember that your needs may change as you grow older—ensure that your new location will be able to deliver and satisfy those needs. For example, moving to a hot and sunny climate may be wonderful whilst you can enjoy swimming, walking, etc., but are the health and social services adequate should you require to use them? A foreign location may mean that your pension and capital may make you a 'millionaire' whilst the cost of living in that country is low—however political change and inflation can convert millionaires to paupers. During your third-age period of perhaps 30 years the nature of a country may change considerably—for either better or worse.

Type of accommodation

If on balance a move seems the most sensible step, the next task is to decide on the type of accommodation. Again, it will be necessary to pay attention to your possible future needs, for example, should you acquire any disabilities. Remember that well-designed aids to living should not be obtrusive and should not embarrass or offend any able-bodied person. It should be possible to ignore them if they are not required—however, should the need for their use arise, they will be instantly available and familiar.

The following are important principles to keep in mind.

1. A single level is better than multiple levels.

2. Sufficient space should be available for your possessions and visitors.

3. Avoid large empty spaces.

4. If not located on the ground floor, make sure there is at least one lift.

5. Go for ease of maintenance and heating.

6. Seek good communications.

7. Ensure convenient access for others.

Generally a flat or bungalow is best but also consider houses where you could live on the ground floor alone, if necessary, for example, where there is a downstairs bathroom and lavatory. Storage space should be ample but convenient, i.e. not overhead. Good communication should encompass not only the availability of a telephone and personal alarm system, but also easy access to public transport and facilities such as shops, banks, and post office. Always remember that there is the risk that you may have to give up your driving licence for health or financial reasons.

Make access easy for others by opting for accommodation in the centre of a community—be it town, village, or neighbourhood. If you ever need support from others, your chances will be enhanced by being conviently located.

With the development and increased use of technology, it should become less necessary for elderly people to move house. If somebody already lives in suitable accommodation with provision of a personal alarm to summon help when needed in an emergency, it should obviate the need to move if and when support is needed. However, should an older person desire special accommodation there is now a greater range available both for purchase and for renting.

Specialized accommodation usually takes the form of sheltered housing. This is based on the almshouse layout. Small, convenient living units are grouped and supervised by a warden. There is the opportunity for mutual support amongst the residents—but this may not occur if they only have their fears and anxieties in common. They will have been brought together to be sheltered and are frequently reluctant to participate in any neighbour's care. If a unit in a private sheltered scheme is to be purchased it is important that professional and legal advice is sought concerning the terms and conditions. Important aspects needing consideration are the management arrangements, especially of the warden and deputy, and the control of service costs and limitations on tenure and resale.

Those who become very frail and no longer have the ability or will to live independently will have to consider institutional care (Fig. 4.1). Essentially this high-dependency form of care is subdivided into residential or rest-home care, and nursing homes or long-stay hospitals. The former concentrates on providing hotel-type services for those who are personally independent or need only minimal help with activities such as dressing or bathing. Nursing homes and hospitals cater for the more disabled and will provide constant nursing supervision and help. The private provision of both residential and nursing home care has more than doubled in the United Kingdom over the last seven years. Some state provision is still available through the local authority for

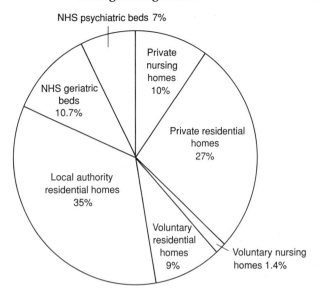

Fig. 4.1 Where elderly people in institutions live in England (1985–6).

residential care and the National Health Service for nursing home and hospital care. However, there has been a contraction in the statutory provision of these forms of support during recent years.

A further development in the private sector has been the establishment of continuing care communities. These provide a full range of accommodation, from totally independent units for those who require no assistance, through sheltered accommodation, to full nursing home care. It is necessary to buy into these schemes and the price is high—but once in, there should be a guarantee that you will be provided with whatever level of care you need for the management of your health and disability problems right up to your death.

Who to live with

For many elderly people there is no choice in this matter, for they find that through death and bereavement they are left living alone. This is particularly true for married women who can now expect to spend the end of their lives as widows. Generally, the older you become the more likely you are to have to face the prospect of

Table 4.4   Household structure of elderly people in UK. (OCPS 1982)

Single elderly woman	27%
Single elderly man	7%
Living with spouse only	45%
Living with other elderly people only	4%
Living with younger people	18%

living alone. If the thought of living alone is intolerable, then the alternatives must be considered. Would it be possible for you to live with a son, daughter, other relative, or a friend (Table 4.4)? However, such cohabitation would only work if your previous relationship with that person was good. If you did not get on well together before the onset of your problems (whether poor health, disability, or bereavement) the situation in the future will not be better and may be considerably worse. The views and opinions of other people, for example, your son or daughter-in-law or the grandchildren, also have to be taken into consideration. When no family solution is available and you have no friend with whom you could share your life, then the forms of communal living described above should be considered—but do not make a permanent and irreversible move until you have tried a new lifestyle.

Where to live in your old age is a very difficult and personal problem. There is no simple or universal answer. Each must make up his or her own mind. However, decide carefully and only after full investigation of all the possibilities. Do not act hastily and especially at times of crisis, such as illness or bereavement. Do not cut off your means of retreat, just in case you find you have made an error.

5   Physical disability

Disability

It is now customary to divide the long-term effects of disease into three categories. *Impairment* is the loss or abnormality of structure or function, such as a weak leg and arm following a stroke. *Disability* is the resulting loss of ability to perform an activity in the normal manner, so that the stroke victim is unable to drive and has a diminished ability to walk. *Handicap* is the ensuing disadvantage in terms of the fulfilment of the individual's role—in the case of someone in his 60s or 70s, this may well be in employment or leisure pursuits or possibly in charitable or committee work; in the case of someone in his 70s or 80s, the enjoyment of a varied and full life and the running of the house and garden. Here, however, we will use the term disability to embrace all these unfortunate consequences of the disease process.

The term disability is a difficult one to define. For example, it has been suggested that almost one in three people over the age of 80 is housebound. This does not necessarily mean that all these people are incapable of walking outdoors or finding their way about, although in many cases mobility and vision may be somewhat restricted. Withdrawal from the outside world often seems to be precipitated by an event which significantly alters the subject's perception of herself so that she now regards herself as old and frail. Examples of such events include falling over in a public place, bereavement, a spell in hospital, or being mugged or merely insulted. Other factors may contribute, such as incontinence, urgency (Chapter 15), and anxiety.

A recent survey has shown that almost 14 per cent of all adults in private households in the UK have one or more disabilities, and in 44 per cent of these the degree of disability is in the more severe half of the spectrum. Almost 70 per cent of all disabled adults are aged 60 or more, and nearly half are over 70. Of those most severely affected, 41 per cent are 80 or over. More old women (75 or over) than old men are incapacitated, even allowing for the different numbers of the two sexes in this age group.

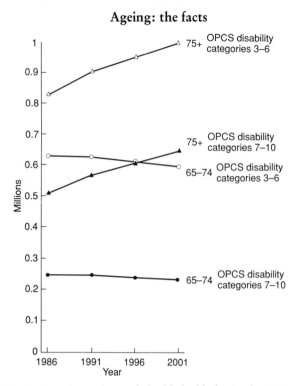

Fig. 5.1 Projected numbers of disabled elderly in the UK ranked in severity from 1–10.

Source of categories for classification of disability by severity: OPCS disability survey.

In all developed countries the rate of disability rises steeply with age, and will continue to do so (Fig. 5.1). Table 5.1 gives a down-to-earth account of the day-to-day effects of disability among old people. The diseases, or impairments, causing these disabilities are numerous and many of them very common, although often causing little or no disability.

Inability to cope with household chores

Many people experience difficulty in managing housework and cooking. Restricted mobility and poor vision are once again often to blame, and it will be readily appreciated that someone who is unable to move about without grasping support with both hands, will find it difficult to cook or even wash up. Weakness or

Table 5.1 Disabilities among 1121 people from East Anglia (UK) aged 75 and over.

Function	%
Unable to cook main meals	35
Unable to shop	36
Difficulty getting about home	24
Difficulty with stairs or steps	50
Unable to do stairs/steps at all or only with help	19
Need help cutting toenails	44
Medium or high dependency due to visual loss	8
Medium or high dependency through hearing loss	7.5
Incontinence of urine	13

Source: Kemp, F. (1985). Survey of the elderly at home, *Occasional paper 14*. Department of Community Medicine, University of Cambridge

deformity of the upper limb will also render cooking and house-work extremely laborious. The task of keeping the house clean is often carried out by relatives, even if the handicapped person lives alone, but failing that, the services of a home care assistant three or four times a week should be sufficient and meals on wheels should be available most weekdays. The exact type and title of the services provided varies from place to place and, in the USA, from state to state, where some community projects are funded under the Older Americans Act. All these services are 'prosthetic' (replacement) rather than 'therapeutic' (enabling the client to perform the task himself). Many people would much prefer the latter, and there is a wide range of gadgets and modifications available to circumvent some of the problems we have been discussing.

Severely reduced mobility: being wheelchair-bound

Even when the ability to walk usefully has been lost, dignity and an independent existence can be maintained in your own home if your arms and hands retain their function. This makes it possible to transfer between bed, wheelchair, and toilet, and also permits operation of the self-propelled type of wheelchair. Electric models are also available, which can be controlled by a single knob and these are very helpful where one arm is affected and the other too weak to propel a one-sided chair. Following a full assessment, this kind of chair can help to make life worthwhile for those who have only made partial recoveries from their strokes.

People with severe arthritis affecting both hips may become completely fixed and incapable of any movement of these joints. It does not require a great feat of the imagination to appreciate that this makes the process of rising from a chair laborious and hazardous, and a 'spring-lift' (or 'ejector') seat may be required. Once up, some of these people can get about with the help of a frame, but others are unable to do so and become wheelchair-bound. Life is more difficult for them than for those with one good leg to bear their weight while transferring. Often, however, the arms are both fully functional. In any event, numerous adaptations around the home are likely to be needed so that kitchen and bathroom activities can be carried out at wheelchair level.

Difficulty with basic activities of self-care

The basic activities of self-care include washing, feeding, dressing, and toileting oneself. Being dependent on help from others during meals or on the lavatory is particularly injurious to the pride, but may become inevitable through a combination of disabilities. Once again, there are devices to make these tasks possible, and the community occupational therapist can advise about these and about various adaptations to the home, which are installed by local authority staff. Some of the adaptations are unobtrusive enough to be good design features in any housing designed for older people. Here are a few examples:

Grab-rails—lavatory, bathroom, stairs;
raised toilet seat;
chair and bed height adjusted;
ramps to replace steps;
electric sockets raised 1 m (3 feet) from floor;
stair lift;
lever taps (coloured red/blue);
door-bell, telephone-bell wired to flashing lights for the deaf;
toilet-paper holder with serrated edge for one-handed tearing;
toilet-paper single sheet dispenser.

Disability to this degree may well necessitate frequent attention from others in connection with the normal bodily functions, and in the UK, after a period of six months this will qualify for the attendance allowance payable to people in their own homes or in nursing homes. Repeated or prolonged attention at night or continual supervision in order to avoid danger to oneself or others also qualifies. The allowance is tax-free and non-means-tested. The UK invalid care allowance, which is taxable, is payable to men and single women of working age who cannot work because they look after a severely disabled person who is receiving an attendance allowance. Services for the frail elderly at home in the USA may be provided by the Home Medical Service or by the Social Health Maintenance Organisation, which is largely financed through Medicare or Medicaid. The Supplementary Security Income is means-tested but may be available to over 65, blind, and disabled people.

Some specific problems

Mobility

A short leg, due to hip disease or a fractured thighbone (femur), leads to a limping gait (putting the ball of the foot but not the toe to the ground), and may ultimately damage the spine. A built-up heel will help to correct the gait. A walking stick of the correct height can relieve the affected leg of 50 per cent of the weight of the body, and if it is attached by a wrist strap, the hand is liberated for other uses when not actually walking. Those who are more impaired often find two sticks necessary, while those who have partially recovered from strokes derive greater support from a quadrupod. The Zimmer walking frame is extremely useful if both hands are strong enough to grip it, and it can be fitted with a carrying basket; many hardy souls use them in the streets having overcome their initial reluctance to accept such an obvious badge of infirmity. Indoors, the walking frame can be rather unwieldy in confined spaces cluttered with furniture. About 60 per cent of stroke survivors manage to get about with one or other of these aids—half of the others walk unaided, and half do not walk at all.

Speech

Profound speech defects occasionally persist indefinitely after a stroke, but 'stroke clubs' can do much to foster communication despite this impairment. These are usually self-help ventures, but can generally be located through the hospital speech therapist.

Availability of aids and appliances

Unfortunately, in the UK aids and appliances are at present supplied through a bewildering variety of channels, although the government White Paper 'Caring for People' may conceivably lead to rationalization.

1. The Red Cross Society, through its local branches, lends commodes, bedpans, urinals, and sometimes wheelchairs.

2. The social services department of the local authority supplies items of a non-nursing nature in connection with mobility and kitchen activities. It is responsible for compiling a register of disabled people under the Chronically Sick and Disabled Persons Act of 1970 but refusal to be entered on this register does not disqualify from assistance of a financial or practical nature. The department employs domiciliary occupational therapists and social workers, and provides a range of supportive home services.

3. The district health authority provides aids to home nursing like incontinence sheets and pads and ripple mattresses, and is responsible for running the community nursing service.

4. The National Health Service, through the Disablement Services Authority, supplies wheelchairs, mobile chairs, and accessories.

5. The family doctor or the hospital consultant prescribes medical and surgical appliances.

Further information may be obtained from the addresses listed in the appendix, and it is well worth seeking advice from the local branch of Age Concern, the Citizens' Advice Bureau, or a disabled living centre.

6 Servicing an ageing society in the UK

An ageing population certainly poses considerable challenges for the health and social services. Fortunately most elderly people live happy, healthy, and independent lives. However it has to be accepted that increasing age does bring an increasing risk of disability and illness. Most ill people in the United Kingdom are old—but most old people are not ill or disabled!

The UK Health Service and elderly people

National Health Service community services

Practically everybody in the United Kingdom can name their general practitioner (family doctor). Most elderly people have consulted the same general practitioner for many years. Feelings of respect and loyalty are often shared by both GP (general practitioner) and patient within the National Health Service (NHS). Having dealt with each other over many years, there are many common bonds between doctor and patient (and the latter's family). At times of stress it is not uncommon for the patient's GP to be the most frequent visitor to an old person's home.

The annual review system

The new NHS contract between general practitioners and their patients has tried to strengthen these ties. Each GP must now offer all their patients over 75 years of age an annual consultation which may take place either at the surgery or in the patient's own home. The patient may decide the venue, but the GP may delegate the task to another member of the primary care team. Community nurses, practice nurses, and health visitors are becoming involved in this system of regular review. It is generally agreed that the annual review should concentrate on functional abilities, for example, asking whether you can hear properly, see properly, walk without difficulty, and control bladder and bowels. If the interviewer detects a difficulty then arrangements can be made for a more thorough investigation and examination so that the underlying cause may be identified and hopefully corrected.

Community nurses

Sometimes still known by their previous title of district nurses, these hardworking people often develop a very close and intimate relationship with disabled, elderly people living in their own homes. They spend about 80 per cent of their time caring for the elderly. They change wound dressings, for example on leg ulcers, and they give treatments, such as injections, enemata or catheter care in a patient's own home. Simpler, but equally important tasks, such as bathing, may be delegated to a nursing auxiliary, but a qualified nurse will still retain a supervisory and supportive role.

If a frail, elderly person has made their permanent home in a residential home (either run privately of by a local authority) then the community nurse may still tend to their needs in such a setting. However residents in private nursing homes must look to the nursing staff of their new place of residence and should not need to receive help from the community nursing service.

Health visitors

These are highly trained nurses who specialize in health education and disease prevention. They are part of the NHS community-services. Unfortunately, they concentrate mainly on children under the age of five years and their mothers. Apart from a few specialist health visitors, their availability to elderly patients is very limited and accounts for less than 20 per cent of their time. This is most unfortunate but is unlikely to change unless there is a marked increase in the numbers of health visitors or a significant re-direction of their efforts.

Domiciliary physiotherapists

These are another very scarce NHS resource—but they may be available in your area. They are physiotherapists who treat patients in their own homes. Exercises can be taught and simple treatments given, but more complicated procedures will necessitate visiting a hospital department of physiotherapy.

Community chiropody

Again, this is more evident by its underprovision than its ready availability. Foot-care by this service may be given in health centres or, if necessary, in your own home. Unfortunately an inadequate level of service often forces people to seek help from private chiropodists. However, not all such practitioners are properly registered and any patient seeking such help must take care.

Community dental services

The most familiar form is the NHS dentist practising from his own surgery. Arrangements can be made for housebound patients to be visited in their own homes. If more specialist treatment is needed it may be available from special hospital dental services. Because of success in the preventive dental care of young people, the dental service is now finding itself with more time available to take on elderly patients. Special training courses are available to increase dental skills in matters relating to dentistry in older people. If you have special needs, ask your health authority if a specialist dental officer is available in your area.

Opticians

If you cannot get to an optician, some will agree to visit you in your own home to check your vision and give advice. Charges are now made for routine eye tests, even for pensioners, although there are some exceptions, such as people with a family history of glaucoma.

NHS hospital based services

No patient should be denied hospital care on the basis of age alone. All departments (except paediatrics and obstetrics) treat elderly people and about one half of all hospital beds are occupied by people of pensionable age. The elderly are also heavy users of out-patient and casualty services. Referral to an appropriate department should be made through consultation with your general practitioner.

The department of geriatric medicine

This is the only hospital department exclusively committed to the health problems of old age. It will always be staffed by doctors, nurses, and therapists who have a special interest and training in age-related illnesses. An effective department of geriatric medicine will provide acute assessment services to respond to emergencies. It will also run an efficient out-patient service for less urgent medical problems. There will also be rehabilitation services—for both in-patients and out-patients, with the latter usually best provided by a day hospital. The day hospital will also be a suitable setting for some assessment work.

The department of geriatric medicine will also provide some continuing care facilities for those patients who are unable to make a sufficiently good recovery from their illnesses and disabilities to leave hospital. Arrangements should also be available for respite care for severely disabled elderly people who are normally depend-ent on members of their family or circle of friends. These facilities should also include both day care services and in-patient beds.

Whilst an in-patient in a department of geriatric medicine, any patient can still take advantage of the services of other hospital departments, when appropriate. There will be unrestricted access to X-ray and laboratory services, and also the opinion of other specialist physicians and surgeons should their help and advice be needed.

All NHS hospital services are currently free of charge but after a six week in-patient stay the state pension of any patient is severely reduced to a small personal allowance to cover incidental expenses alone. If there are financial problems the social work department will be able to advise.

Private health insurance

Health care in old age is expensive. Special insurance schemes are available for elderly people and tax incentives are currently available to increase their attractiveness. However, not all schemes are as comprehensive as one would wish. Great care is needed in scruti-nizing the small print in any insurance scheme, and you would be well advised to seek help from your family and general practitioner before committing yourself to any expense. Important exclusions can often include previous illnesses and their consequences and any commitment to provide long-term care should it become necessary.

Local authority services for elderly people in the UK

These consist predominantly of community services but some residential provision (rest homes) is available. Although it has been official UK government policy for nearly 30 years to provide effective community care, the resources available remain inadequate. There had been an expectation that the situation would have improved by 1991 with the passage of the NHS and Community Care Bill. Unfortunately, parts of the Community Care Bill have been postponed. The main force of the Bill is to identify the local authority as the prime provider of community care. There are serious anxieties that the practice may never replace the theory and that the provision of community care will remain patchy and thin. Charges are usually made for local authority services, unlike NHS services which remain predominantly free at the time of use.

Community care assistants

These are the keystones of statutory community care and are still known to most people as 'home helps'. They are employed and trained by the social services department of the local authority. The contribution they make to maintaining frail, elderly people in their own homes is only surpassed by the work of informal carers (relatives and friends). Initially set up as the service providing domestic help, its emphasis has gradually been changing. More recently the community care assistants have been playing a large role in providing personal care. They now help people to dress in the morning and to get ready to go to bed at night. They also help with bathing and personal hygiene. Their functions are therefore increasingly overlapping with those of the community nursing service. As a consequence, it has been suggested that the two services could be sensibly combined, but this has not yet happened.

Peripatetic wardens

It is now possible to have the benefit of the supervision of a warden—even if you continue to live in your own home. This has been made possible by the development of body-worn personal alarms. When activated the alarm will put you in touch with a warden or control centre which can then provide assistance. Some systems have voice contact; others rely on alarm systems alone. These services are usually arranged through the local authority housing department. Initially they were only available to tenants of council accommodation, but have now been extended to include owner-occupiers. Privately arranged and financed schemes are also available. Your local authority housing department or department of social services should be able to provide you with local details.

Help with meals

The meals on wheels service in the UK is well established. Initially set up by the Women's Royal Voluntary Service (WRVS), it is now in many instances supported or taken over by the local authority social services department. The service provides disabled people with a hot, midday meal in their own home. This can usually only be provided a few times a week, but a daily service is sometimes available. A more attractive alternative for some people is to attend a luncheon club. However, availability or ability to use transport may make attendance difficult for many elderly people. The great advantage of attending a lunch club or day centre which provides a meal is that the food is eaten in the company of others. When necessary, community care assistants will help with both shopping and cooking, and thus help to provide meals for people living in their own homes.

Help with transport

Special transport is often part of the package of care when a place is offered at a day centre or a luncheon club. Volunteer car services and specialized ambulance transport can be arranged for attendance at hospitals, clinics, health centres, and day hospitals. Special transport arrangements are also available in some areas. Subsidized or adapted cars and taxis can be available to help disabled people to visit family and friends, or to travel to keep other appointment,s for shopping expeditions, and so on. Details will be available from your local authority social services department.

Home aids and adaptations

If disabilities impede activities of daily living, such as dressing, bathing, and food preparation, then help and advice is available. The local authority employs domiciliary occupational therapists who can visit you in your own home. They can assess your problems and provide aids and adaptations to help you to maintain your independence.

When community care is no longer possible

In this sad situation great tact and skill are needed to make alternative arrangements (Chapter 4). It is essential that a full assessment is made of your problems and needs and all possible ways of improving the situation are explored before you agree to give up your own home. The help of family, friends, doctors, nurses, therapists, and social workers may be needed to help you make the right decision about your future.

7 The biology of ageing

What is ageing?

The word 'ageing' is used in two main senses whether it is applied to a man or to his motor car. The simpler sense is purely chronological and tells us that it is becoming a period of many years since he or it was first taken home from the labour ward or factory by proud new possessors. The second describes the many changes which have taken place since then, some readily apparent to the eye of the beholder, others perhaps not even easily detected on examination of the component parts. There is also a third sense in which the word is used when applied to biological systems, in order to indicate the processes by which the first sense has led to the second. These processes have to explain the fact that the longer we live after reaching our peak, the more universal and the more strongly developed are the decremental changes of structure and function which render increasingly precarious our hold on life. These explanations are the field of enquiry of gerontologists, who are pursuing them at an increasingly fundamental level—from the organism down to the cell and ultimately to the molecule. There is, in addition, a further sense in which the word is used when applied to a population, and that is to describe the change in its composition whereby an increasing proportion of individuals of that population are advanced in years.

Even when we are old, many of the cells of the body are still being replaced by new ones through continuous division. These include the blood cells and those of the skin and the lining of the gut. Other cells grow old with us because they rarely, if at all, undergo division. Examples of these are to be found in the kidney, brain, heart muscle, and the lens of the eye, and once we have received our complement of them, those that are destroyed can never be replaced. Clearly these different types of cell will exhibit very different ageing phenomena, and these will in turn have different effects on the ageing of the organism.

Age-related cellular changes

Various changes have been described in ageing cells, such as a variation in the number of chromosomes (aneuploidy) and the accumulation of inert waste material or 'clinker' in the form of a 'wear and tear' pigment called lipofuscin in nerve, kidney, liver, and muscle cells where it interferes with energy release and affects function.

Animal tissue transplantation experiments have shown that some tissues can be transplanted time and again and so outlive not only the original donor but also a series of recipients. *In vitro* studies have yielded even more striking and informative results. Certain human cell lines can be cultured in perpetuity, but only if they are abnormal (cancerous). In the 1960s and 1970s, Hayflick, worked with normal human embryonic fibroblasts, the relatively simple cells that produce the fibrous skeleton of our connective tissue. He showed that there seemed to be a fixed limit to the number of divisions that these cells were capable of, although there was a fair amount of individual variation. The upper limit was 50, give or take ten either way, but if the cells were taken from mature subjects the capacity for reduplication was reduced, although to an extent correlating poorly with the age of the donor. Cells frozen in liquid nitrogen for over 20 years apparently retain a 'memory' of the number of divisions they are still due to undergo following reconstitution. Towards the limit of their potential span, these fibroblasts acquire certain attributes shared by ageing and malignant cells, such as aneuploidy. Hayflick's work points convincingly towards the existence of a biological clock which ticks by at a certain pre-ordained rate.

What sets the clock?

It is well known to the life insurance industry that the genes exert a major influence on ageing and longevity. He who would live to a ripe old age would do well to choose his parents wisely, and different animal species, as we shall see, age at vastly different rates. Down's syndrome is a genetic disorder characterized by the presence of an extra chromosome number 21, and people with this condition show some signs of accelerated ageing, including the deposition in the brain of amyloid composed of the same protein fragment as is found in the age-related dementia of Alzheimer's disease. The gene encoding the amyloid protein is located on chromosome 21—in very close proximity to the gene which transmits the rare familial form of Alzheimer's disease.

What stops the clock?

Each animal cell contains over 200 million protein molecules, each of which has been assembled from amino acids according to a precise pattern specified by DNA (deoxyribonucleic acid), the material which stores genetic information, and acts as a programme or blueprint. The template for protein synthesis is transmitted from the DNA in the nucleus to the cytoplasm in the form of smaller, readily transported messenger molecules called RNA (ribonucleic acid) which link with protein to form complexes called ribosomes where the protein molecules are assembled. The DNA and the ribosomes have to be intact in order that protein synthesis can proceed and the cell continue to undergo division.

Should any errors develop in the transcription of information from DNA to RNA or its onward relay to the protein molecule on the assembly line, a strain of abnormal and defective protein (whether structural or enzyme) would emerge. Such errors probably do not arise simply as a result of advancing age, but they can be caused by a number of environmental factors, including heat, cold, ultraviolet light, irradiation, free oxygen ('superoxide') radicals, and even glucose. An accumulation of environmentally mediated errors over the years could result in the production of more and more lines of defective protein and malfunctioning or non-replicating cells. The mechanisms for detecting and repairing or eliminating these errors may become less efficient as the organism ages.

During cell division, alterations occasionally take place in the structure of a chromosome which may be fairly gross or may affect a single gene *locus* or a few neighbouring gene *loci*. These alterations, called mutations, occur particularly as a result of irradiation and other harmful stimuli, but can also occur on a spontaneous basis. Mutations fundamentally affect the DNA and thus the encoded information, and this is one of the mechanisms whereby environmental factors influence the integrity of the cell, the tissue, and thus the organism.

Ageing of connective tissues

Everyday experience enables us to detect the difference in the texture of veal and beef, and the distinctive properties of perished rubber and old glue or plastic. These physical changes also characterize ageing connective tissue, which becomes stiff and loses its previous elasticity. This is thought to be due to chemical cross-linkages which form bridges between adjacent collagen molecules, accounting for the features we observe in the skin, tendons, and muscle sheaths as we grow older. Other physical changes are caused by proteins in the lens of the eye, called crystallins, which become joined together by increasing numbers of disulphide bonds during the formation of a cataract.

Ageing of the organism—homeostasis

Homeostasis is the series of mechanisms by which the body retains its chemical composition and its physical characteristics despite changing external conditions and despite variations in intake of fluid and salts. These mechanisms depend on the autonomic nervous system and on the kidneys, among other organs. The capacity to maintain homeostasis seems to be impaired in the frail elderly, who become much more liable to hypothermia and falls in blood pressure and to loss of body water. Indeed the ability of the kidney to conserve water has been thought to decline steadily throughout adult life, although this belief is currently being disputed.

Immunity and ageing

The efficiency of the immune system shows a distinct tendency to decline in old age, as was tragically illustrated by the Christmas 1989 influenza epidemic in the UK. This decline probably also contributes to the increasing prevalence among the old of diseases, other than infections, including cancer. Galen regarded the involution (wasting) of the thymus, an organ situated near the heart, as the earliest sign of ageing. This process commences in childhood, and the blood cells (T-lymphocytes) which are processed in the thymus and which are vital constituents of the immune system, function less well in old people. Animals who are subjected to the removal of the thymus age rapidly and die early.

Ageing and the species

Ageing and death are necessary for the survival of a species which has to some extent contained random loss through natural disaster. It is perhaps unlikely that ageing is an evolutionary adaptation since elderly individuals are so uncommon in wild animal populations that living space for newcomers is seldom at a premium. It is more probable that ageing is an aspect of evolutionary neglect of the latter half of life: for species where environmental mortality is high, the species will invest its resources in reproductive effort rather than in the detection and repair of errors. Reproduction depends not only on reproductive function, but also on the remainder of the body being capable of developing, foraging, and fighting, as well as repairing itself in the short term. Larger animals, on the whole, live longer than smaller ones—it takes time to grow big (see Table 7.1).

Table 7.1   Maximum recorded longevities of various animals in years.

Tarantula spider	11–20
Carolina box tortoise	129
Bird (sulphur-crested cockatoo)	80
Mouse	38–40 months
Elephant (Asiatic)	78
Horse	over 40
Man	120

Decline of function with age

It must be repeatedly emphasized that many of the parameters we measure and which are reported to decline in older people may do so for three reasons—ageing itself, an increasing prevalence of age-related disease, and disuse due to an inactive lifestyle—and that those reasons can only be teased apart if studies are carried out longitudinally on disease-free subjects rather than cross-sectionally on different cohorts. It is becoming clear that many measurements of physical and mental ability which have been accepted as showing inevitable deterioration do not necessarily do so, or at least the

Table 7.2 Some anatomical and functional variables in a 70-year-old man, expressed as a percentage of values in the young adult.

Function	Percentage of young adult
Arterial oxygen pressure	90
Total body water	87
Cerebral blood flow	80
Kidney weight	80
Maximum heart rate	76
Resting oxygen consumption	74
Muscle mass	74
Maximum oxygen consumption	65
Resting cardiac output	64
Maximum urinary concentration	64
Kidney blood flow	60
Cardiac reserve	50

Source: Kenney, R. A. (1985). Physiology of Aging. *Clinics in Geriatric Medicine*, **1**, 37–59.

deterioration does not set in as early as has been thought; and that in the case of those relating to physical fitness, the deterioration can be so influenced by conditioning that many a 70-year-old emerges as fitter than sedentary people half his age. The data shown in Table 7.2 should be regarded, therefore, with considerable caution.

8 'Normal' ageing

Whatever steps we take to stay 'young', the combined effects of biological ageing and adverse environmental influences eventually declare themselves. As mature adults, around the age of 25, we experience maximum physical, sexual, and reproductive capacity. Decline thereafter is so gradual that for many years we are unaware of 'getting older' unless greatly stretched. Up to the age of 50 or 60 we may enjoy a period of great functional stability, the menopause excepted. However in our late 60s and 70s the cumulative effects of ageing become obvious, even to ourselves! The precise rate of ageing depends upon genetic inheritance modified by circumstances such as early nurture, behaviour (lifestyle), and environment. Older people differ so much that the reader will be aware of plenty of exceptions to the general descriptions offered here. Death almost always comes from some readily recognizable disease or trauma rather than old age itself.

Changes in appearance, behaviour, and function

Our behaviour and looks give others a good indication of our age; they can estimate it to within five or ten years. The quality of the skin, greying and loss of the body hair (Chapter 17), changes in body contours, and the stance and facility of movement are obvious clues. Elderly people tend to stand with the knees and hips slightly flexed and with a little stoop. There is an increased tendency to sway because of less effective postural support responses. Walking is characteristically slowed, with shorter, broader-based steps and reduced arm swing. More time is spent in 'double support' (both feet in contact with the ground) as gait velocity is reduced. When there is much anxiety or the going becomes more difficult, as on rough or slippery ground, stairs, or in congested places, movement becomes especially hesitant.

Body composition and function

As people grow older there is a gradual reduction of all active tissues, including brain, heart, lungs, liver, kidney, muscles, and bone. By middle age some decrease in muscle power and stamina must be accepted, and even athletes cannot compete on equal terms with those 15–20 years younger. In many sports the middle-aged are regarded as 'veterans', for example at 40 years for women and 45 for men in tennis. Persistent exercise slows down the rate of muscle and bone loss but seems unable to prevent it altogether. By age 80 most people have lost about half their muscle mass and replaced it by fat. Provided this does not increase weight overall, the gradual increase in fat is not harmful, and in truth its presence can prevent an otherwise scrawny appearance.

The general chemical activity (metabolism) of the body, which is highest in infancy, also declines throughout life. To avoid putting on too much fat it is necessary to reduce food intake from middle age onwards, even for the physically active. If you take very little exercise, your energy requirement at absolute rest actually accounts for most of your energy requirement. Since most of the energy in food is in fats and carbohydrates (and in alcohol for those who drink it liberally), these especially must be curtailed. The intake of fresh fruit and vegetables should be maintained.

Changes in function

An imperceptible decline in many functions affects us after the age of 25–30 years. By middle age there are measurable declines in vision, hearing, and the speed of response to mental and physical challenge. Physical stamina (but not sight or hearing) can be maintained to a considerable extent by keeping active.

Ageing of the nervous system

The nervous system has an unique role in our ability to function at both a social and a biological level. In our 60s and 70s we all suffer some slowing of the thought processes and some impairment of memory ('benign senescent forgetfulnes') but nevertheless can cope well with all we need to do. Loss of active cells and of supporting tissue affects some areas of the brain much more markedly than others. Fortunately, reserve capacity is so great that cell loss solely from ageing appears to cause little embarrassment.

Malfunction rather than just loss of cells accounts for much of the trouble with an aged brain. This may be due to inadequate production of neurotransmitters. These substances transmit signals from one nerve cell, or neurone, to another, and so from one part of the brain to another. Neurotransmitters also permit brain cells to communicate, via neurones in the spinal cord and peripheral nerves, with different parts of the body, including muscle, bone, and skin. The integrity of the nervous system is vital to the maintenance of homeostasis, or constancy of the internal bodily environment in the face of external change (see Chapter 7).

Vision

Loss of elasticity of the lens of the eye occurs progressively throughout life and by middle age most of us are aware that reading books, newspapers, etc. is increasingly difficult. Spectacles may be needed for the first time and either bifocal or multifocal lenses may be required. Colour discrimination becomes less good and adaptation to darkness is also impaired, which affects night driving. In the home and in public places good levels of illumination and bold contrasts of light and dark are required to allow for safety in movement and especially to avoid hazards such as changes in floor level (see Chapter 17).

Hearing

Hearing also deteriorates, especially for high-pitched sounds but it is not clear how much of this can be attributed to trauma from the noisy environment. The loss is detectable by special tests years before we ourselves become aware of it, usually in middle age. It is not the loudness of the spoken word which is the problem so much as lack of definition of each separate word. The words sound 'fluffy' because consonants, which are high-pitched sounds, are not properly heard. Background noise compounds these hearing difficulties, so that conversation while travelling or in groups is particularly tiresome. Reduced direction-finding for sounds and poor comprehension of frequently interrupted speech make for extra difficulty in general conversation.

New names of people or places are demanding because the context offers no clues ('Was it Mrs McCave or Mrs McCabe who telephoned?'). Names such as these can be virtually indistinguishable, yet some people find it embarrassing to ask the caller to spell

out the name slowly, distinctly, and preferably using the inter-
national phonetic voice procedure (i.e., Mike Charlie, Charlie,
Alpha Bravo Echo) or a homely variant. Much of the problem of
comprehension relates to slower data processing in the brain,
therefore unhurried speech is better heard. Fast talkers tend to blurr
their consonants and run words into one another which frustrates
elderly listeners (see Chapter 17).

Balance

The eye and ear both have to do with balance but neither is crucial
in keeping us on our feet. Furthermore, the ability to maintain an
upright posture may fail even with quite good eyes and ears. The
vestibular (balance) part of the ear shows a less severe functional
decline than the cochlear (hearing) part. However complaints of
dizziness have been observed to be more common in older subjects,
affecting about 40 per cent of men and 60 per cent of women over
the age of 65 years.

Balance becomes less secure in later life. To stay on our feet we
depend upon the integrity of many different parts of the brain and
spinal cord, as well as on sensory inputs from mechanoreceptors
which detect movement in the muscles and joints. Weakness or
stiffness in the muscles or joints further impairs posture control
and especially the ability to correct sudden displacements from the
upright position. Adequate vision does aid balance but in the dark
this compensation fails. Nevertheless, most falls occur during the
day when we are up and about (Chapter 13).

Heart and circulation

The capacity for pumping blood around the body is reduced at rest
and during exercise. However those participating in regular strenu-
ous activity preserve more of their exercise capacity. Blood pressure
tends to be higher in older, westernized people but not in all
cultures. After the age of about 70 the pressure tends to level off
and it is not entirely clear why this is so. One possibility is that
those with the higher pressures have already died from stroke, heart
disease, or other cardiovascular disorder (see Chapter 16).

Lungs

As age increases, our lungs and chest wall become less elastic and
our maximum breathing capacity is reduced. The mechanisms

protecting the lungs from infection, such as ciliary action and normal mucus production, become less effective making us more liable to chest infection. There is less efficient gas (such as oxygen and carbon dioxide) exchange in the tiny air spaces (alveoli) of the lungs. For a given level of physical effort, we have to breathe much harder to maintain a satisfactory blood oxygen level. Not surprisingly, elderly people become breathless more quickly on exercise. They are readily upset by a lack of oxygen and show adverse effects to high altitude more quickly or, if not acclimatized, at a lower level, for example at 2100 metres (less than 7000 feet). Age changes in the lungs are all greatly overshadowed by the adverse efects of cigarette smoking and atmospheric pollution (see Chapter 16).

Kidneys

The kidneys shrink as we age. Each kidney consists of numerous subunits called nephrons which collectively cleanse the blood of impurities. This collective function of the nephrons declines, as does the blood supply to the kidneys; additionally, the nephrons die off. As a result of these changes, renal function in old age may be markedly impaired. This is not normally troublesome but when illness strikes, poor kidney function can cause major problems (see Chapter 15).

Sex in later life

Sexuality is a lifelong feature of our lives, but with increasing age the sexual responses wane and usually in the 60s and 70s the frequency of sexual activity is much reduced. However the notion of sexless older people is a myth: the elderly still have sexual dreams, fantasies, and hopes. Of course human sexuality is much more than just an affair of the genitals, of intercourse, and procreation. Every one has an innate desire to love and be loved; but to give expression to these feelings requires an appropriate partner, and emotional deprivation occurs in many older people living alone, especially widows.

At the menopause, menstruation, ovulation, and reproduction cease but sexual expression need not be affected and indeed some women report an increase in libido at this time. Men do not have this abrupt loss of fertility because manufacture of sperm continues. Vasocongestive responses of the erectile tissues of the genitalia in both sexes are less intense and the speed of arousal is slower, more noticeably so in men. Men need active stimulation to become erect, the erection takes longer to develop, is less turgid than formerly, and may reach full tumescence only at ejaculation. The male orgasm may be delayed, the volume of ejaculate is reduced, and the recovery time before further coitus is possible is prolonged for hours or even until another day. In women, nipple erection remains satisfactory but vaginal lubrication is delayed and reduced. Orgasmic contractions are reduced in strength and number and resolution is quicker.

To use a mountaineering metaphor, sex in late life, like all aspects of human endeavour, is more to do with the pleasure of pottering around in the foothills than racing for ever higher peaks of achievement. In this more leisurely context erectile failure should not necessarily mean the end of sexual activity. Nevertheless any serious sexual problem, male or female, should be discussed with your family doctor because there may be a simple means of help available. Alternative strategies can also be developed to enable sexual satisfaction for both partners if that is what they wish.

Regularity of expression and good health are the keys to lasting sexual responsiveness in both sexes and the authors advocate continued use of the marital double bed. With an active and willing partner, many elderly people continue to enjoy their sexual relationships. Sadly by the age of 80, women outnumber men by two to one and this poses insuperable problems in a rigidly monogamous society. A lengthening of male life expectancy could do wonders for the contentment of elderly women. Alternatively, farsighted young women might chose to marry men younger than themselves—the opposite of current practice.

Attempts to control human ageing

The fundamental mechanisms of ageing are not known and cannot yet be controlled. Despite this ignorance, attempts to control ageing have a very long history. Some are based on philosophy and psychology, such as meditation; others are more physical, with exercise, use of electricity, special diets, 'taking the waters', or consuming far-fetched potions reckoned to have near magical properties (see Table 8.1).

Although there is no 'elixir of life', there is much we can do to

Table 8.1 Some attempts at rejuvenation and life extension.

	Examples
Plant products:	Mandrake, orchids, ginseng, yohimbine, aromatherapy, essential oils (e.g. evening primrose oil)
Animal products:	Shellfish, eggs, semen, cantharides, royal jelly, soured milk
Water cures:	The legendary Prester John and the Fountain of Youth, spas, and hydrotherapy
Electrical contrivances:	Galvanism, electromagnetism
Notable twentieth century remedies and their promoters	Gondal extract injections: Charles E. Brown-Sequard Treatment of intestinal intoxication: Elie Metchnikoff Vasectomy: Eugen Steinach Monkey testicular grafts: Serge Voronoff Serum therapy: Alexander Bogolomets Cellular therapy: Paul Niehans Procaine therapy: Anna Aslan

improve our chances of worthwhile longevity. We should take care to avoid accidents on the street, at work, in sport, or in the home and abstain from substance abuse such as of alcohol, tobacco, and medicines. Sensible precautions should be taken to avoid infections such as influenza, venereal diseases including HIV infection (AIDS), food poisoning, tetanus, and malaria. An optimistic out-look is valuable, because a happy mind promotes a healthy body and the reverse also appears to be true, in that those who are chronically anxious or depressed do tend to suffer more from physical illness.

Physical exercise and an appropriate diet are important at all ages as is stressed elsewhere in this and other chapters. Much of what is commonly regarded as being the result of ageing may in fact be due to progressive disuse. For example, stamina, strength, suppleness, balance, and bone mass are all reduced with ageing but they wane very much less quickly if adequate exercise is taken. The ideal is to maintain fitness throughout life but most of us have a 'fitness gap'—a gap between our present level of fitness and the level we could achieve even taking into account our age, disabilities, and existing diseases.

If it can be managed, some increase in exercise will be beneficial. For most people aged 50 and over, regular brisk walking (brisk by your own standards), thrice weekly or better still daily, provides a training effect improving general health and stamina. In part this may be due to reduction of obesity which occurs if you are overweight unless you replace the expended energy by eating more! The extra energy consumption occurs not only while exercising but for some time afterwards while you recover from your exertions. Additional benefit comes from the sense of well-being which the exercise produces and from the reduced risk of coronary heart disease and maintenance of bone strength.

Drugs to prolong active life

Apart from adhering to the canons of healthy living, what else can be done to preserve vitality and promote longevity? Probably not very much, for despite the claims made for many different anti-ageing drugs, the authors are not convinced of the value of any of them with the singular exception of hormone replacement therapy (HRT). None the less mention is made of a few other contenders in this field.

Hormone replacement therapy (HRT)

At the time of the menopause the level of circulating oestrogen is much reduced. This may lead to embarrassing circulatory upsets or 'hot flushes' and night sweats which usually respond to hormone treatment. There may be symptoms of anxiety, irritability, head-ache, insomnia, and even mental depression. Later there is genital atrophy with vaginal dryness which impedes sexual activity, accel-erated bone loss, and an increased risk of vascular disease. The increased cardiovascular risk and weakening of bone pose serious threats to elderly women. Given proper selection and medical supervision, HRT can not only preserve some essential feminine characteristics but can also reduce the risks of fracture and vascular disease (see Chapter 13).

Ginseng

Ginseng has been in use, especially in the Far East, for around 2000 years. The name 'jen-shen' means 'man-root' because the root has human resemblance. This anthropomorphism may account for the attribution of magical properties to extracts from the plant! Ginseng glycosides are mildly stimulant, alleviating fatigue and helping to combat stress. There is no evidence that ginseng increases longevity. When too big a dose is taken nervousness, insomnia, irritability, and raised blood pressure occur.

Gerovital (GH3 or KH3)

This preparation has achieved world fame on the basis of very slender evidence. It is essentially procaine hydrochloride, commonly used as a local anaesthetic. Unsubstantiated claims are made for it as a treatment for some of the disorders of ageing and as an anti-ageing agent.

Vitamin E

Vitamin E is another drug claimed to have anti-aging properties and to promote sexual potency, physical endurance, and lessening of the likelihood of heart attacks. The evidence is not scientifically robust but as with ginseng the absence of sound evidence does nothing to dent the vast market for vitamin E. Both substances are well marketed in the multi-million pound health and beauty industry. Vitamin E is present in abundance in the average Western diet in many vegetables, vegetable oils, and whole grain cereals.

'We live as long as God has ordained, but there is a great difference between living wretchedly, like poor dogs, and being well and vigorous'

Goethe.

9 The body's chemical and physical composition

Age-related changes

As we pass from youth through middle age and on into old age, there is a diminution in the lean body mass (LBM). This process starts at about 25 years of age and entails a reduction in our protein content—there is less meat in us, less bone, and the solid internal organs such as kidneys and brain tend to shrink. Obviously, if we stay the same weight, our muscles are being replaced by fat, so it is healthier to lose weight as we age even if commoner to gain it! A man of 75 kg at the age of 25 has a LBM of 61 kg and he contains 13 kg of fat, but at the age of 65 his LBM is 49 kg and his content of *matière grasse* is 28 kg (Fig. 9.1.)

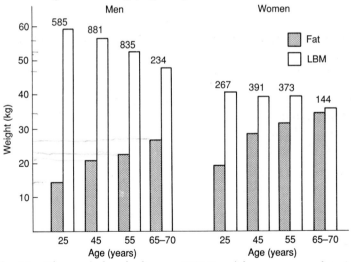

Fig. 9.1 Changes in lean body mass (LBM) and fat content as a function of average age in men and women. The number of subjects at each age is shown above the bar graphs.

Source: Conrad, K. A. and Bressler, R. (1982). *Drug therapy for the elderly*. CV Mosby, St Louis.

There is also a tendency to lose water, so for once stereotyping has a scientific basis and we really do become desiccated. The water content of an embryo is approximately 90 per cent, but it has fallen to 80 per cent at birth, to 70 per cent at age 20, and to 60 per cent or less in old age. It is thought that most of the loss is from inside the cells rather than from the tissue spaces.

Is the chemical balance maintained in old age?

One of the fundamental characteristics of the ageing organism is loss of adaptability. Our capacity to maintain a constant internal environment in the face of external environmental changes and challenges deteriorates. This capacity, most highly developed in warm-blooded creatures, is called homeostasis. Homeostasis depends on many organs, but principally perhaps the kidneys and the autonomic nervous system, both of which are liable to decline in function in old age and especially in certain diseases such as diabetes mellitus.

Ageing and the kidney

Each minute rather more than a litre of blood is pumped through the kidneys and about a tenth of it passes through the 650 000 miniscule filters or glomeruli into the tubules which eventually lead to the collecting system and the bladder. In a fit, young person, this means that about 130 ml of plasma are processed and enter the tubules each minute, although eventually only around 1 ml of urine is produced each minute, the remainder of the water being reab-sorbed into the circulation. The amount of urine production, the quantity of water eliminated from the blood stream, and the composition of the urine in terms of salt, potassium, and other elements are manipulated by the tubules in such a way as to keep the body's balance under precise regulation. Each glomerulus and its tube is called a nephron, and conventional wisdom has it that by the time we reach 80, half of them have been lost, so the quantity of plasma processed per minute is halved. Despite this, it is also widely accepted that 80-year-olds are more prone to dehydration because the tubules they still have are much less capable of returning water to the blood stream and they will continue to produce large quantities of urine even if they do not drink much fluid. However they also have difficulty eliminating surplus water, salt, and waste products such as urea.

As we pass through life our kidneys are exposed to damage by atherosclerosis and especially by high blood pressure, as well as diabetes and cystitis and many other common diseases. The generally accepted view of declining renal function may be very misleading, as it includes subjects with well-defined common disorders, and a third of people probably do not show this steady decline in renal function with the passage of the years.

Why are old people liable to dehydration?

We have seen that one reason is the deterioration in kidney function that many, if not necessarily all old people suffer. There are, however, other mechanisms involved in maintaining the water level of the body, for instance, the sensation of thirst which prompts us to drink. There is evidence that this mechanism often does not work so well, or is less sensitive to minor degrees of water depletion, in many elderly people. In addition, people may ignore the sensation of thirst because of depression, or immobility, or swallowing disorders, or because they are afraid of needing to empty the bladder at a socially inconvenient time. Finally, many elderly people are prescribed diuretic tablets for fluid overload, and if taken on a long-term basis these can seriously deplete the body of water, sodium, and potassium. Excessive quantities of urine are also produced in certain diseases such as diabetes.

What is is like to be dehydrated?

Failure to drink enough leads to predominant water deficiency and the portion of the body's fluid mainly affected is that within the cells, typically leading to thirst and eventually to weakness and confusion. But if quantities of fluid are lost through vomiting, diarrhoea, or excessive urine excretion, there is variable loss of salt, water, and potassium, and this mixture is often partially replaced by drinking water or other fluids containing inadequate quantities of electrolyte. This leads to depletion of the portion of the body's fluid in the tissue spaces and eventually to a fall in the circulating blood volume. This form of dehydration accompanied by salt loss is much less likely to evoke the sensation of thirst. It results in profound weakness and dizziness caused by a fall in blood pressure,

and contributes to the sunken eyes and pinched cheeks so characteristic of grave illness.

Is it common to be water-logged?

We are all familiar with the puffy, swollen ankles so often associated
with advancing years. If you press with a finger on such an ankle,
it will leave a dent as the fluid in the underlying tissue is displaced;
if it does not, the ankle is simply fat. This accumulation of fluid
used to be called dropsy and afflicted such celebrities as Henry
VIII. It is associated in the medical mind with chronic heart failure
and too often results in prescriptions for diuretics which, if brisk in
action, can convert fluid in the ankles to urine in the slippers. The
fluid also accumulates in the lungs in acute heart failure and causes
severe breathlessness.

There are many others causes of fluid accumulation in the feet and
legs, and the commonest is perhaps simply sitting in a chair all day,
when the effect of gravity is combined with a lack of muscular
activity which normally helps pump the blood back to the heart.
Many of us have experienced arriving at our destination after a long
flight with swelling of the feet and ankles, and here an additional
factor is the pressure of the seat on the veins in the thigh and at the
back of the knee. There is a small but real danger that this pressure
may not only compress the veins but actually encourage the
formation of blood clots, or thromboses, within them. By the time
the hapless airline passengers are prized out of their cramped
battery-chicken-class seats and massaged out of the rigid Z-shape
into which their bodies have congealed, they may have developed
not only pressure sores and jet lag but ankle swelling and venous
thrombosis as well! Sound health advice for anyone of middle age or
beyond who is contemplating a long airline flight would be to watch
a travel programme on the television instead. To sound a slightly
more positive note, it helps to stretch the legs and walk to the toilet
from time to time, and it also helps to choose a fairly empty flight or
to pay the considerable extra cost for a first-class ticket.

A venous thrombosis is certainly another cause of swollen ankles,
but this is usually confined to one leg. When both are affected,
other conditions which need to be considered include kidney
diseases which limit water excretion and, more commonly, certain
drugs which can have the same effect, including steroids and many
anti-inflammatory drugs used in the treatment of arthritis.

Diabetes

Diabetes both accelerates age-related changes and is itself, to a certain extent, an age-related decrement of chemical balance. Diabetes is an inability to keep the blood-sugar level within the normal range. Over the age of 70, 20 per cent of men and 30 per cent of women show an impairment of glucose homeostasis and about 10 per cent can be regarded as diabetic. A few have been diabetic since early adult life or even childhood, but most of them will have a maturity-onset type of diabetes which is especially common in obese people and is usually manageable without insulin, being controlled by diet alone or diet together with tablets. The onset may be quite symptomless or there may be a vague deterioration in the general health: sometimes there is thirst, weight loss, and a tendency to pass large quantities of urine; sometimes there may also be a susceptibility to infection particularly of the bladder, and itching around the genitalia.

Treatment

If there are symptoms, treatment will probably be required, and the first step is the dietary correction of obesity. In those who are not particularly overweight, or whose symptoms persist following reduction, it is usual to prescribe a controlled diet in which, these days, most of the energy requirement is supplied in the form of carbohydrate rather than fat. The carbohydrate should be of the high-fibre, unrefined polysaccharide type to be found in wholemeal bread and biscuits, wholegrain breakfast cereals (porridge, Weetabix, Shredded Wheat), all vegetables (especially pulses and potatoes in their jackets), all fruit, and brown rice. Monosaccharides (glucose) and disaccharides (sucrose) should be avoided, which precludes syrup, honey, jam, marmalade, chocolate (including the 'diabetic' variety which is both high in calories and expensive), sweets, cakes, pastries, ordinary biscuits, sweet drinks, tinned fruits, and sweetened cereals. Fairly strict dietary control provides a basis for achieving a reasonably stable blood-sugar level in a substantial number of diabetics. Other diabetics require tablets which stimulate the secretion of insulin by the pancreas (sulphonylureas), and a few need a different type of oral drug as well or instead (biguanides).

Urine testing

Although patients are usually advised to test the urine regularly in order to check the control of their diabetes, the amount of sugar in the urine is often a very inaccurate guide to the blood level, and a blood-sugar measurement is advisable from time to time and is essential for those on insulin. Any acute illness is likely to disturb diabetic control, as can diuretic drugs given to disperse accumulated fluid in other conditions such as heart failure. A simple device for obtaining a drop of blood from the finger is now available, and there is a small instrument (glucometer) to be kept at home so that patients can undertake their own measurements.

The autonomic nervous system (ANS)

The autonomic nervous system (ANS) is that part of the nervous system that regulates the activities of parts of the body not generally subject to direct conscious control, such as the intestine, the heart and blood vessels, certain glands such as sweat and salivary glands, and the pupil of the eye. Some of its functions, such as the act of emptying the bladder, seem to be under conscious control and yet the contraction of the muscle of the bladder is not a deliberate act in the same way as the contraction of a muscle of the hand is, for example.

Why is ANS failure important?

A great many reflexes are mediated through the ANS, and diseases such as diabetes and Parkinson's disease which commonly affect the central nervous system (CNS) may be associated with failure of these reflexes. If you suddenly leap out of bed first thing in the morning, perhaps bursting to empty your bladder, your blood vessels will be widely dilated but they rapidly constrict to prevent pooling of blood in the lower extremities and a catastrophic fall in blood pressure. Even if the pressure does fall, blood flow through the brain is selectively maintained in order to preserve consciousness. People, usually elderly, suffering from postural hypotension due to non-functioning of these reflexes are liable to feet faint and to collapse. Other causes of postural hypotension include varicose veins, loss of circulating blood volume, and certain drugs, notably antidepressants, tranquillizers, antihypertensives, and drugs used to treat Parkinson's disease.

How does ANS failure cause hypothermia?

Hypothermia occurs when the body temperature falls below 35 °C (95 °F). The three main causative factors are serious illness (such as sustaining a stroke and lying on the floor all night unable to move), a cold environment, and ANS malfunction. Not all these factors need to operate and, for example, immersion in cold water after a shipwreck will induce hypothermia in previously fit young people. If we are cold, we reduce heat loss by controlling the blood vessels in the skin and reducing the blood flow through our surface layer, and we increase heat production by shivering. Both these reflex reactions are impaired if the ANS is not working properly and the core: periphery temperature gradient is lost. In people who have become hypothermic, it has also been found that there is often a failure to register minor changes in ambient temperature so that they fail to put on extra clothing, close windows, or light fires.

How dangerous is cold weather?

Hypothermia kills, and prevention is certainly better than cure. The home should be kept warm and it is unnecessary to observe the deeply entrenched British habit of opening bedroom windows at night. Half the body's heat loss occurs through the scalp, so a woolly nightcap makes a useful and not unduly extravagant Christmas present for an aged relative. Hypothermia does represent a very fundamental failure of homeostasis, reducing us to the same level of helplessness as the cold-blooded animals. Indeed, the rigid limbs and the sluggishness of thought and movement of a hypothermic patient are reminiscent of a lizard in the cold of the morning before the sun has started to warm its tissues and activate its chemical reactions. Hypothermia does not, contrary to the popular press, invariably indicate a callous failure by society to protect its frailer members: nor does it usually involve a great deal of suffering, as victims of hypothermia seldom complain of feeling cold if conscious and never if unconscious. The main principle in the treatment is to rewarm the patient in a gradual and controlled way, but there are many complications and the mortality is high except in mild cases.

In an average (pre-global warming) winter in England and Wales there are about 40 000 deaths in excess of those to be expected during a similar period of time during other seasons, but these are mainly due to strokes and heart attacks related to changes, induced by exposure to cold, in the blood and blood pressure rather than to hypothermia. Curiously enough a similar phenomenon has been noted during heatwaves.

Homeostatic failure

If there is a single feature which is the hallmark of the medicine of old age, it is this tendency for homeostatic mechanisms to become less efficient. Our bodies are too finely tuned to tolerate swings of temperature, pressure, or chemical make-up. Failure of homeostasis is the main reason why illnesses, accidents, or surgical operations from which a young and otherwise healthy adult would recover quickly, may be life-threatening to an aged person.

10   The ageing brain

As our years increase, the size of our brain decreases: unpalatable, but true. By the age of 80, the human brain weights about 100 grams (7–8 per cent) less than it did in our 20s. Brain cells, or neurons, are not replaced when they die, and throughout the lifespan we are estimated to lose 50 000 of them a day. That may sound pretty serious, but we do start with some ten billion of them so that a lifetime's loss is only about 3 per cent of the original total. In any case, the rate of loss varies between different areas of the cerebral cortex (grey matter), being greatest in the upper part of the temporal lobe and the hindmost part of the frontal lobe. This 'neuronal fallout' is paralleled by a depletion in parts of the cortex of some of the chemical messengers (neurotransmitters) which carry the impulse from one nerve cell to another across the tiny clefts (synapses) which separate them. It has been suggested that it is the number of interconnections between the cells, rather than the number of cells, which is important. It has also been claimed that the number of these connections can be increased in rats by training them in a maze, with the result that the weight of the forebrain and the length and width of the cortex become greater. This appears to be true of rats reared in an intellectually deprived environment, whose brains start off greatly disadvantaged by comparison with those of their siblings which have been intellectually stimulated from birth, and whose brains show no such response to training.

Little granules of a yellowish-brown pigment called lipofuscin accumulate in neuronal cell bodies and this material is thought to represent a waste product. Similarly, starting at around age 60, microscopical examination of the brain will reveal so-called 'senile plaques' of degenerated cells and other waste matter scattered throughout the cortex.

These changes to the structure of the brain that accompany the passage of the years are reflected in various physiological measurements, such as the tendency for the frequency of the normal alpha waves of the electroencephalogram (EEG) to become significantly lower. Another example is the flow of blood through the brain which is widely accepted as showing a reduction of about 20 to 25 per cent between ages 30 and 70. However, a cautionary note must be sounded here. The studies on which this information is based are cross-sectional, i.e. they comprise groups of people of different ages all assessed at the same time, and may include numbers of unhealthy individuals who may distort their results. Indeed, it is very difficult to see how a longitudinal study (testing and retesting the same individuals over a long period of time) of the structure of the brain could ever be conducted in human beings.

The other parts of the nervous system

The brain sends messages down the spinal cord to the various segments of the body and receives messages coming up the cord from them: the brain and the spinal cord are known as the central nervous system (CNS). The nerves which branch out from the cord to instruct the muscles to contract, or to receive various sensory signals from the skin and also from deeper organs are called the peripheral nerves. The speed of conduction of an impulse along a nerve is usually thought to be about 15 per cent lower in a person of 80 than in someone of 30. The physical reaction involved in jamming on the brakes in a car requires you to see the oncoming vehicle, transmit that message a few centimetres to the brain, make a judgement about the right thing to do, and send an impulse down the spinal cord which is then relayed down the sciatic nerve to the big muscle at the back of the calf telling it to contract and thereby depress the brake pedal. It is very difficult to make all the measurements necessary to tease apart the various components of this rather complex process, but it is probable that what takes the most time is the central function of evaluating the information in the brain and forming a decision to act on the basis of that information. The speed of this central component appears to decline more with age than that of the transmission of the signal down the sciatic nerve. The received wisdom is that the overall reaction time is 30–40 per cent longer in old age. The example chosen was a fairly simple one, and the reactions required in sporting activities such as tennis involve more complex responses, for example turning, running, and operating the racket arm. In elderly subjects who take regular exercise the total reaction time has been found to be similar to that in younger individuals and faster than in sedentary people of the same age.

Does the brain deteriorate in later life?

There has been a wealth of experimental work on the testing of intelligence at various ages, much of which is hampered by the difficulty of defining intelligence in any universally acceptable terms except 'that quality which is measured by intelligence tests'! And although many and various are the tests which have been designed to assess 'mental ability' or intelligence quotient (IQ), their use among older people is further bedevilled by the fact that they are usually primarily intended for use among children and adolescents. In tests incorporating practical information more appropriate to the lifestyle and culture of older people, it is often found that scores *increase* with age.

More than almost any other investigation, IQ comparisons at different ages require longitudinal repetitions rather than cross-sectional surveys. If different age-groups are compared, they will represent groups of people separated by huge differences of cultural background in terms of education, experience, expectations, way of life, media exposure, and habits, and are thus not comparable. Longitudinal studies in which the same individuals are retested over long periods of time overcome these objections but clearly present formidable practical difficulties.

Plasticity

Nevertheless, some studies of this type have been conducted. In one so-called 'cross-sequential' investigation, the same subjects were re-assessed seven and fourteen years after initial testing, and at the same time new subjects of all ages were introduced into the survey and assessed at the seventh and fourteenth years. The outcome suggested that, on the whole, there was a significant degree of decline after the age of 67, and this became substantial between the ages of 74 and 81. But differences between individual subjects were as large as differences due to ageing, and there were also tremendous individual differences in the rate of change (Fig. 10.1).

This characteristic of ageing is known as 'plasticity' and applies to most physical and mental attributes. Similar studies have shown

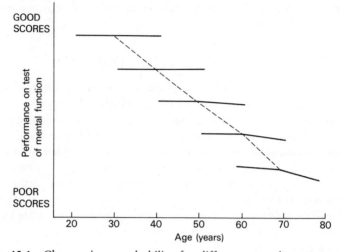

Fig. 10.1 Changes in mental ability for different age cohorts (groups); because younger cohorts begin at a higher level, cross-sectional comparisons (*dashed line*) give an exaggerated impression of mental deterioration with advancing age.

Source: Huppert, F. A. (1982). *Geriatric Medicine*, **XII**, 32–7.

that *all* age groups actually improve their own performance on retesting, and training has been shown to produce an improvement in standard tests of fluid intelligence even in the eighth decade.

Some recent research in Cambridge illustrates some of these points. An elderly group was compared to a young group in a whole batch of tests of learning, memory, reaction time, and decision-making, and found to perform less well. But the range was so much larger in the older subjects that in each test many of them did better than the average for the young people (mainly undergraduates), and quite often one of the older ones would actually come top. There was thus a great deal of overlap, and it was generally found that the elderly people who performed badly were in poor health. Perhaps it is worth briefly looking at some specific characteristics.

Speed

Between the ages of 20 and 60, the reaction time seems to fall by an average of 20 per cent in tasks of psychomotor function involving, for example, pressing the correct button in response to flashing lights of different colours. This appears to be due to slower decision-making in the brain, and not to changes in the peripheral motor or sensory systems. The older subjects seem to opt for accuracy rather than speed, and take longer in order to ensure that the response is correct. There is again, a tremendous overlap between the age groups, and speed is particularly affected by ill-health, but some decline appears to be usual from the 50s on.

Problem-solving

Once again, on the whole the older subjects are less successful at solving complex problems. It is arguable whether this is due to lower IQ, to slower information processing, or to greater rigidity of thought. It is said that fluid ability declines, but crystallized ability improves with age. What is clear is that the elderly are more easily 'thrown' by the inclusion of irrelevant and redundant information. It has been demonstrated that older engineering workers have more difficulty interpreting involved working drawings.

Attention

Tests of vigilance often indicate that attention is maintained at as high a level in older subjects as in younger ones until fatigue sets in at a rather earlier point. Distractability is generally greater among older people: it is everyday experience that we more readily lose the thread of a programme on the car radio when the traffic thickens or there is a somewhat stressful junction. The alternative is selective inattention to the road, which is why we advise older motorists against a car radio or a loquacious companion.

Memory

Some differences between the ages have been shown by cross-sectional studies and are therefore open to doubt. There may be a deficit in short-term memory as demonstrated by recall procedures, which involve retrieval as well as the initial reception and storage. This is much less apparent when recognition of a recently displayed pattern only is involved and does not require retrieval. Remote memory remains relatively unimpaired, but, contrary to popular belief, is *not* necessarily better than in the young.

Conclusions

Cross-sectional studies merely illustrate the increasing pace of socio-cultural change which is now beginning to render people obsolescent in their 50s!

Performance testing does show some decline, but this is due to a variety of factors. In the elderly, it is easily adversely affected by fatigue. It is also affected by cautiousness, so that many do not perform to their full potential due to extraneous factors. For instance, it has been shown that there is little reduction in the ability to hear and understand sentences between the 20s and the 70s so long as the listening conditions are favourable. If the hearing conditions are poor, people experience difficulties in their 30s which become marked in the 50s.

There seems to be some decline in intellectual function which does *not* begin early, does *not* affect all aspects of the intelligence, and is *not* universal and inevitable in all the elderly. From the early 60s to the mid-70s, there is normally a decline in some but *not* all abilities in some but *not* all people. After the age of 80, however, a decline is the rule.

In one Australian study, 80 people between 63 and 91 received weekly German lessons. After three months, half of them passed an examination normally attempted by schoolchildren after a three year course. We have no direct evidence that continued use of the mental faculties ensures the preservation of mental health, but it certainly cannot be bad for the health, and it certainly can enrich our later years.

Personality

Once again, many widely held beliefs are founded on extremely shaky evidence. Once again, the questionnaires in use are often more appropriate for young students than for those of mature years. It is, therefore, with some reservations that one accepts the theory that advancing years are characterized by increasing introversion and that this leads to a form of adjustment to frailty and approaching death by disengagement from others and from many of the world's activities. Perhaps it should be looked upon more accurately as a means of adaptation to the rejection and exclusion which society offers to its older members, and to the role which seems to be required of a 'good' old person—undemanding and no trouble to anybody.

On the whole, the capacity for adaptation among the elderly is underestimated. What *is* true is that they are less inclined to take risks, and a degree of rigidity is to be found. And another generalization which seems to be reasonably true is that the young regard the present as better than the past, and the future as probably better than the present, whereas in our 60s they are all equally well regarded, but when we reach our 70s the past seems to be the best, then the present, with the future probably worse than either.

Older professionals, it has been found, are better than their junior colleagues at conserving time and energy and at distinguishing between critical and peripheral tasks. Their needs regarding achievement may have been satisfied, but the need for recognition and a sense of personal worth persists. Men, it is claimed, become more passive, women more assertive in their pursuits.

Requirements for psychological health

These have been summarized as follows:

  (1) an adequate standard of living;
  (2) financial and emotional security;
  (3) health;
  (4) regular and frequent social interaction;
  (5) the pursuit of personal interests.

These requirements are no different from those of younger age groups, and they may not seem very ambitious, but unfortunately they are not all readily attainable for large numbers of the very old, frail, and bereaved.

Sleep

Various studies have shown that complaints of insomnia are more prevalent in older subjects (26 per cent in one report, 45 per cent in another). Difficulty in getting off to sleep is one problem, and although the average time taken by a younger adult is ten minutes, at the age of 70 it is 20–25 minutes. Frequent waking is also common, and these periods of wakefulness may be prolonged. At the physiological level, it appears that the total time spent asleep diminishes in old age but not dramatically so; the old spend more time awake in bed, and there is a significant reduction in what is variously called stage four, delta wave, or slow wave sleep (from the appearance of the electroencephalogram), which is the state of deepest sleep when arousal is most difficult. This may be why sleep often seems less refreshing when we grow older. Nevertheless, older people generally awaken abruptly, unlike the young who seem to engage in a prolonged struggle to reach the surface. An elderly person who is awakened during or immediately after a period of rapid eye movement (shallow) sleep is much less likely to be able to recall a dream than a younger person. An older man has fewer and less complete nocturnal erections when compared with a younger one.

When discussing samples of older people, it must always be remembered that such samples will contain a higher proportion of persons suffering from some major or minor disorder. Although disruption of sleep may simply be due to daytime napping, it may therefore also be related to conditions which cause pain or discomfort, or which necessitate getting up to pass urine, as well as constipation, depression, or anxiety. Some simple guidelines for better sleep include rising at a regular hour, being active during the day, maintaining a comfortable temperature in the bedroom, avoiding coffee or tea during the evening or, for that matter, going to bed hungry. Also avoid worrying. This may sound easier said than done, but one of the few rules in medicine with scarcely an exception, is that people do not die or even become seriously ill through insomnia. A detective novel or a radio or television show late at night may reduce mental activity and the degree of arousal, and a warm milky drink often has a very helpful effect. Only as a last resort is a short course of a mild hypnotic drug occasionally justified, but when taken for more than two to four weeks these drugs may lose their effect or accumulate in the body and cause somnolence, confusion, unsteadiness, or habituation.

There is some evidence that snoring is commoner in later life, mainly due to various types of nasal obstruction. Smoking and obesity are likely to make this tendency worse. There is no simple cure, but the problem is worth mentioning as it can contribute to marital disharmony. When lying on the back, snoring is occasionally followed by a variable period when the breathing stops altogether, and this can occasionally cause daytime drowsiness and other symptoms.

Restless legs syndrome

A maddening but usually benign condition which can severely disrupt sleep is the 'restless legs syndrome' in which an intolerable creeping sensation affects the lower legs during the evening and particularly in bed at night. There is a compulsion to keep moving the legs and this affords some relief although some sufferers find they have to get out of bed and walk about. The cause, in most cases, remains obscure although it occasionally seems to be associated with iron deficiency or with defective arteries or nerves in the legs. It is a very difficult condition to relieve, although there are drugs (such as levodopa) which are reported to be helpful sometimes.

11 Age-related psychiatric problems

The psychiatry of later life is equated in the public mind with dementia, and although the dementing illnesses do dominate the field in old age and particularly in the 80s and beyond, there are numerous other problems which can occur over a considerable age range. Perhaps we should start by looking at some of those areas which are not necessarily pathological before considering serious disease states.

Self-neglect

Most of us are familiar with people who, although they do not necessarily live alone, have created an environment which we would not regard as being particularly hygienic. This is by no means the sole prerogative of elderly people, as the bedrooms of some teenage children or some of the flats shared by groups of students demonstrate. Nevertheless there is perhaps a tendency for most people to lead relatively orderly lives throughout middle age, even if some retain a certain disregard for conventional standards of neatness of house, garden, clothing, or person. In later life this variation becomes more marked, and elderly people are sometimes encountered living in conditions of extreme degradation with total neglect of appearance and hygiene. This state of so-called 'senile squalor' is quite often the cumulative result of a degree of lifelong eccentricity, the lack of structure that follows retirement, and the isolation that may follow bereavement. Depression and poverty can further reduce the chances of any action being taken to break the vicious circle.

There is a subdivision of this unfortunate group of people who, although perfectly lucid, positively hoard rubbish and surround themselves with piles of newspapers or old baked bean tins so that the house becomes crammed and access to different rooms is through narrow tunnels. This is sometimes called the Diogenes

Syndrome in recognition of the Greek philospher's total disregard for social niceties although his dwelling, a barrel, was more notable for the absence of personal possessions than their accumulation. The geriatrician who coined this title recalls rehearsing his lecture aloud prior to its delivery and being told by his wife that if it was not for her, he too would have sunk into an identical lifestyle. A familiar fictional character who exhibits some of the features described is Charles Dickens' Miss Haversham.

Alcoholism

Alcoholism is the repeated consumption of alcoholic beverages to the extent that it leads to dependency, physical disease, or other harm (World Health Organization 1977) (Table 11.1). It is claimed

Table 11.1   Risk of alcohol consumption (units per week*).

	Women	Men
Low intake Low risk	Up to 14	Up to 21
Moderate intake Intermediate risk	15–35	22–49
High intake High risk	36 or more	50 or more

* 1 unit = 8 g alcohol and is contained in ½ pint beer, 1 glass wine, 1 (smaller) glass sherry, or 1 single whisky or gin

that 5–12 per cent of men and 1–2 per cent of women in their 60s are 'problem drinkers'. They can be divided into the 'graduates', who had been drinking heavily down the years, and the 'late-onset' drinkers who have started heavy consumption in later life, often in response to some life event such as retirement or bereavement, in order to anaesthetize the pain of reality. Elderly drinkers are more inclined to conceal their habit than younger ones, and they are more likely to maintain a constantly high intake rather than to indulge in periodic 'binges'.

    Alcohol misuse can seriously damage the health, perhaps particularly in later life when a reduction in the body water and the lean body mass may lead to higher blood levels after a given dose. The dangers are greatly heightened by the concurrent use of hypnotics, tranquillizers, antidepressants, and certain other drugs.

Among the adverse effects of alcohol is a predisposition to self-neglect and poor hygiene and nutrition. Aches and pains, insomnia, loss of libido, depression, and anxiety may all be caused or aggravated by excessive alcohol and may in turn lead to a misguided search for solace in the bottle. Falls are a further danger, and damage to brain, liver, and nerves frequently follows prolonged misuse. Referral to a drinking problem clinic is advisable as soon as the problem is recognized by the subject.

Hallucinations

An hallucination is the experience of seeing a person, animal, or object when in reality there is nothing there. It is a common experience in later life and does not indicate that the subject is going mad. Hallucinations of the loved one are common following bereavement. Hallucinations are also common among people with visual disorders. Bizarre visions are a common and distressing adverse effect of a number of drugs, notably those given for Parkinson's disease: they are also a feature of alcohol misuse and abrupt withdrawal. They are encountered in association with depression, and also in certain other psychiatric disorders.

Paranoid psychosis

One of these disorders is *paraphrenia*, in which the hallucinations are more often auditory than visual. It is a kind of late-life schizophrenic illness without the same disorder of thought and personality. Delusions of persecution by neighbours or relatives are the rule, and the subject may accuse them of stealing, tampering with walls or doors, sexual molestation, or derogatory remarks. Lonely, unmarried women are most often affected, especially those who are deaf. As with all deluded, hallucinating (or confused) old people, confrontation must be avoided. The response to major tranquillizers is generally good—if the patient can be persuaded to take them.

Depression

Depression is the commonest psychiatric condition in elderly people. The prevalence of severe depression is about 3 per cent among people over the age of 65, but milder degrees probably affect 12–15 per cent of people in this age-group. These milder depressive states are difficult to distinguish from the melancholia which may attend the changes and losses of advancing age. The lowering of mood and loss of pleasure in true depression is however more pervasive and of a different quality to that encountered in normal experience. In severe forms, the sufferers are preoccupied with ruminations of guilt, dread, fear, hopelessness, lack of self-worth, and anxiety in what has been called a 'ceaseless roundabout'. There is apparent apathy and loss of spontaneity, and frequently there are deluded thoughts relating, for instance, to real or imagined physical disease, so that physical symptoms are common. Restlessness and agitation are other common manifestations in old people, and another form of depression is characterized by an apparent lack of orientation that may lead to the suspicion of dementia.

Losses and physical illnesses may precipitate true depression, as can certain drugs. In most cases, the cause is not clearly known, although genetic factors may play a part. There is thought to be a neurochemical abnormality caused by the underactivity of certain neurons which are dependent on amines such as noradrenaline and serotonin for transmission of impulses from one nerve cell to another. Antidepressant drugs achieve their effect by blocking the absorption of these substances into the nerve endings and thus increasing the quantity present in the clefts between the cells.

Depression often leads to ill-health through self-neglect, malnutrition, and dehydration. The most obvious complication, however, is suicide and men over the age of 80 are the highest risk group in the population. Apparent attempts at suicide are, more often than not, unsuccessful in the young: the reverse is true among the old because many live alone and are found too late, and because resuscitation is more difficult. In general, the older the sufferer, the greater the suicide risk, especially among men. Other risk pointers are a family history, a previous serious suicidal attempt, social isolation, bereavement or an anniversary thereof, physical ill health, and hypochondriasis.

The modern drug treatment of depression is often successful. If it is not effective in a particular case, electroconvulsive therapy (ECT) may be life-saving despite its generally bad press. Indeed, many people feel that ECT is a safer and quicker form of treatment than drugs for elderly people gravely afflicted by this dreadful state.

Anxiety states

Anxiety is a common feature of depression, dementia, and physical illness, and often affects persons of all ages, young as well as old, who have none of these things. Sometimes it is permissible to wonder whether it would be normal if the old and frail, the isolated, and the impoverished were *not* anxious, or, for that matter, frankly depressed. Anxiety states occurring in isolation are less common than depressive illness, but may lead to a degree of depression, and may commonly produce physical symptoms such as palpitations, breathlessness, giddiness, and abdominal discomfort. The condition may respond to the doctor's reassurance, or, better still, to the relief of loneliness if this can be achieved. Otherwise, a three or four week course of a minor tranquillizer such as diazepam (Valium) may be useful but the dose should be a low one and never exceeded by the patient. A gentle hypnotic may be required at night, and drugs which can be recommended, with reservations (see p. 78), are chlormethiazole (Heminevrin), dichloralphenazone (Welldorm), and temazepam (Euhypnos).

Institutional neurosis

'Institutional neurosis' is the term given to the state of apathy and passive acceptance found in those consigned by society to long-term care. Now that the days of prolonged residence of young people in mental hospitals are over, the condition has become very much the preserve of the very old, and even today those who visit extended-care geriatric wards may find the inmates sitting round the walls of the day room in silent inactivity—however great the efforts made by the staff and by voluntary workers. This is a powerful argument for delaying, or better still, avoiding custodial care.

Dementia

Dementia is a global impairment of the personality, memory, and intellect without any alteration of conscious level. The commonest form is Alzheimer's disease but another common variety is due to a succession of minor strokes and this is likely to occur in people with a high risk profile for arterial disease from factors such as smoking or poorly controlled hypertension. These two conditions are common in old age and therefore commonly coexist. Other forms of dementia are seen in Parkinson's disease and some other less common neurological conditions, and also in association with alcohol misuse, certain metabolic disorders (vitamin B12 deficiency and hypothyroidism), late syphilis, and AIDS.

Alzheimer's disease is, justifiably, regarded with greater dread than any other disease, for 'to the ageing, dementia is synonymous with loss of dignity'. It is also incurable, progressive, and very common. The figures usually quoted for the prevalence of significant dementia are 2 per cent of people aged between 65 and 75 rising to 20 per cent over the age of 80 (Fig. 11.1).

The condition is eventually totally destructive of the victim as a person, but the onset is insidious and initially impossible to

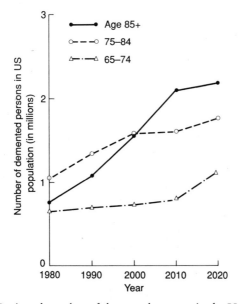

Fig. 11.1 Projected number of demented persons in the United States by age, 1980–2020.

Source: National Institute on Aging, Prevalence Estimates, and US Bureau of the Census (1982). Current population reports, series P–25, No. 922, *Projections of the population of the United States: 1982–2050* (Advance report). US Government Printing Office, Washington DC.

distinguish from the 'benign senescent forgetfulness' to which
everyone becomes prone. The progress is slow but relentless,
starting with impairment of abstract thought and learning ability,
loss of initiative, concentration, interest and business ability, pro-
ceeding to failure of memory—initially short-term, later long-term.
Aimlessness, disinhibition, and deterioration of personal habits
follow, and restlessness, wandering, and disorientation are very
trying for the family of the sufferer. A vegetative state may mark
the final phase, and the whole course of the disease may take up to
ten years. Sadly, all the doctor can offer is a diagnosis and whatever
support he or she can muster.

What causes Alzheimer's disease?

Some authorities believe that Alzheimer's disease merely represents
an acceleration of normal age changes, others regard it as a specific
disease, while yet others view the distinction between disease and
normal ageing as spurious (attempting 'to separate the undefined
from the indefinable'). In Alzheimer's disease, the cortex of the
brain is thin with gross neuronal loss, particularly in the temporal
lobes and certain other areas, including a particular, minute location
in the brain stem. Microscopy reveals that there are many more
senile plaques and neurofibrillary tangles to be seen than in 'normal'
aged brains. There is depletion of some of the transmitter amines
throughout the cortex, but unfortunately, pharmacological man-
oeuvres aimed at enhancing neurotransmitter activity have so far
signally failed to yield as good a response in Alzheimer's disease as
they have in depression and Parkinson's disease.

Useful though these descriptive studies are in clarifying the
clinical manifestations of the disease, they still beg an explanation
of the underlying cause. In a few cases there is a clear genetic basis,
and interestingly, the gene implicated has been located on chromosome 21 which is present in triplicate instead of duplicate in Down's
syndrome (in which features of Alzheimer's disease are prominent
at a relatively early age). Other theories come and go, with
aluminium toxicity having enjoyed a recent temporary resurgence
and a possible slow virus receiving some support from those who
detect parallels with bovine spongiform encephalopathy (mad cow
disease) and the loss of brain function seen in AIDS. Research is
progressing apace into this major cause of suffering, death, disability, and expenditure.

Care of patients with Alzheimer's disease

The earlier stages of the illness may last for as many as seven years and are usually followed by more rapid progress over two or three years culminating in death. It rapidly erodes the capacity to lead an active, independent, decision-making existence so that a great deal of help will be required from the family or from the community services. When behavioural problems such as wandering or nocturnal restlessness become prominent, it may still be possible to support sufferers in their own homes with the help of day care and respite admissions to institutional care. Sadly there is a woeful shortage in the UK of longer term institutional provision for either 'EMI' (elderly mentally infirm, hitherto the responsibility of the local authority social services department) or 'ESMI' (elderly severely mentally infirm, hitherto the responsibility of NHS psychiatric services).

Legal considerations

Mental incompetence as a result of dementia or other illness carries legal implications.

Testamentary capacity

To make a valid will in the UK it is necessary to have testamentary capacity. In general it is also true that a power of attorney can only be valid if the person on whose behalf it is exercised can issue meaningful instructions, and becomes invalid if he or she loses testamentary capacity. An exception now exists in the form of the 'enduring power of attorney', which is drawn up while the person concerned is of sound mind with specific provision that it shall continue to operate even if he or she becomes no longer of sound mind. The law requires that a testator should:

(1) understand the nature of a will;

(2) be conversant with the property to be disposed of;

(3) recognize those who may have moral claims on the property.

The description of Lord Chief Justice Cockburn over a century ago remains just as valid today:

It is essential that the testator shall understand the nature of the act and its effects: shall understand the extent of the property of which he is disposing: shall be able to comprehend and appreciate the claims to which he ought to give effect: and with a view to the latter object, that no disorder of the mind shall poison his affection, prevent his sense of right or prevent the exercise of his natural faculties.

In regard to conventional power of attorney, Lord Justice Brett (1897) stated 'Where such a change occurs to the principal that he can no longer act for himself, the agent whom he has appointed can no longer act for him.'

Court of Protection

If the patient, because of mental incapacity or inability to communicate, cannot manage his own affairs then it is necessary to apply to the Court of Protection (see p. 200). In most cases a receiver will be appointed to act as the patient's agent, usually an interested relative or some other suitable person. When the assets are small the appointment of a receiver may not be necessary but the realization by the patient that his property is being protected by the court often removes a source of worry. The court will require an appropriate medical certificate to state the nature and severity of the illness together with the likely prognosis.

Most of the work of the Court of Protection is to do with elderly people especially those with a dementing illness. The powers of the receiver are strictly controlled; for example, he may not on his own initiative make loans or gifts or dispose of any property or investments but he can and should see to it that the patient is provided with those little extras that add so much flavour to life, such as special foods, drinks, flowers, toilet articles, and clothing.

What about compulsory committal?

Occasionally, relatives, friends, or neighbours are faced with the distasteful decision that an elderly person whose wish is to remain at home should be overruled on grounds of advanced physical or mental infirmity. Depriving someone of his or her liberty is rightly regarded as a step of considerable gravity and usually requires a number of signatories. The details are beyond the scope of this book, but the following is a brief guide of steps that can be taken in the UK:

1. *Physical* incapacity with inadequate care, unable to look after themselves and living in insanitary conditions—Section 47 of the National Assistance Act: Removal to Place of Safety; initiated by social worker or GP, now rarely used.

2. Compulsion to reside in a given place, attend for treatment, and permit access by doctor or social worker on the ground of mental disorder—Section 7 of the Mental Health Act: Guardianship; application by relative or social worker.

3. Compulsory committal to psychiatric hospital—Sections 2, 3, and 4 of the Mental Health Act provide for relatives or social workers to make an application, usually via the GP.

Acute confusion

It has been emphasized that the confusion and disorientation of dementia is of insidious onset and slow progression. It is not uncommon for old people to develop a much more acute variety of confusional state, typically of abrupt onset in a previously totally sane person. This is the acute confusional state or delirium, and is due to some organic physical illness until proved otherwise. The causes are numerous and range from acute physical illness such as pneumonia or septicaemia to poisoning by various drugs in widespread medical use to brain conditions such as non-paralytic stroke. If the cause is identifiable and treatable, restoration to complete competence is a reasonable expectation, though unfortunately not invariably realized.

12 Stroke, Parkinson's disease, and motor neurone disease

What is a stroke?

A stroke is the result of a disturbance of the blood supply to a part of the brain. Each part of the brain has its own function, and those functions contained within the damaged area will be seriously affected. About 15 per cent of strokes are caused by cerebral haemorrhage, which is a rupture of a blood vessel with destruction of brain tissue by the ensuing torrent of blood. A large majority of strokes, about 80 per cent, are caused by the blood supply being drastically diminished by atherosclerosis (resulting in cerebral infarction) with or without the formation of a thrombosis (clot). Sometimes a clot travels upwards from the heart or from an ulcerated area in the carotid artery in the neck. It will be readily appreciated that there are many different kinds of stroke, depending on which of these underlying mechanisms is responsible and on the area of the brain affected. It will also be appreciated that the onset is typically sudden but that the effects are long-lasting. Stroke is a chronic disability with an acute onset.

How common are strokes?

The number of strokes occurring annually per 100 000 population has fallen substantially in the USA and, to a lesser extent, in other developed countries during the past quarter century. Mortality rates have also fallen in these countries but have risen sharply in Eastern Europe. This decline in Western Europe, North America, Australia, and New Zealand seems to have come to an end, so that stroke remains the third leading cause of death after coronary heart disease and lung cancer in the UK. Perhaps more importantly, it continues to cause immeasurable suffering to victims and their families and an enormous amount of dependency and utilization of hospital and nursing-home bed days. Some estimated figures are shown in Table 12.1.

Table 12.1   Some stroke statistics.

Number of strokes p.a. (England and Wales)	102 000
Number of deaths p.a. (UK 1984)	81 838
—as proportion of deaths all causes	12%
Proportion of stroke deaths occurring in people over 65	90%
Proportion of stroke deaths occurring in people over 75	70%
Number of hospital admissions (England 1985)	118 500
Mean duration of stay (weeks)	7
Number of hospital bed days	5 780 000
Proportion of total hospital bed days (third after mental disorder/handicap)	6–11%
Disabled stroke survivors (UK 1971)	130 000
Mortality at one month	17%

What causes stroke?

Cerebral haemorrhage is mainly caused by high blood pressure although a rarer cause is an inborn weakness in the wall of one of the arteries supplying the brain. Cerebral infarction is caused by atherosclerosis but sometimes it is a sudden fall in blood pressure, perhaps due to a heart attack, that reduces a precarious blood supply through a narrowed vessel to a level insufficient to keep that particular part of the brain alive. The main risk factors for atherosclerosis are as follows:

- age
- high blood pressure (and therefore obesity and heavy alcohol use)
- smoking
- diabetes
- raised blood cholesterol.

How is the patient affected?

Cerebral haemorrhage tends to be more catastrophic than infarction and often results in sudden death or in profound unconsciousness for a variable period. Cerebral infarction can also be rapidly fatal or cause loss of consciousness, but it is more typical to find on awaking in the morning that one leg and arm are extremely weak and that standing and walking are impossible, or perhaps that in the middle of tea the face becomes asymmetrical and the speech slurred, and standing or even sitting upright is impossible. This represents the picture of a fairly major stroke, but much less severe patterns are common in which just the speech is affected or only one limb is involved or the weakness is fairly mild.

The commonest type of speech defect following a stroke occurs when the left side of the brain has been damaged in a right-handed person, and consists in an extremely frustrating inability to find words, although such words as are available to the patient are reasonably well articulated since the main mechanisms for pronunciation are preserved. Usually, but not invariably, the spoken word is understood, and it is important not to talk about the victim in his presence as though he were incapable of comprehension.

If the other, non-dominant, side of the brain is damaged, it is common to encounter a curious combination of subtle but profoundly disabling effects, comprising neglect of the affected side of the body and perhaps of the environment as well, loss of body image, and disordered spatial perception. The result can be dramatic, as for instance in the case of a patient who tries to throw the paralysed left arm out of the bed claiming that it belongs to someone else. It may be less dramatic and the patient may simply sit with the left arm 'lost' and dangling under the arm-rest of the chair. Such patients, even if severely paralysed, often strenuously deny that there is anything the matter with the useless arm and leg or indeed that they are in any way unwell. They may, although possessed of perfectly sound vision, be incapable of drawing simple diagrams, or of bisecting a horizontal line anywhere near the middle, tending to totally ignore the left side of the figure. And they may recover the ability to move the limbs only to find themselves unable to dress or to find their way about. The same sort of defect, when affecting the dominant side, can cause difficulty in distinguishing between right and left, and a profound difficulty in performing even the simplest mental arithmetic.

Sensation is sometimes blunted over the paralysed arm and leg or indeed there may be predominant loss of sensation. One of the senses affected may be awareness of the position of the limb, so that it becomes hopelessly clumsy. Another sense quite often affected is vision, but in a very specific way: typically, both eyes lose just half their field of vision—the half containing objects on the same side as the paralysed limbs. Patients are often quite unaware of this and totally fail to notice anyone approaching them from that side.

Other subtle neurological disturbances can occur, but mention should perhaps be made here of three highly adverse effects, all of which may be transient and clear up in a few days or a week or two, or which may be permanent.

1. Mental changes. A stroke may simply cause confusion, but it may also cause permanent impairment of the intellect and personality. Depression, not surprisingly, is exceedingly frequent; epilepsy is not uncommon and may need long-term medication.

2. Urinary incontinence.

3. Difficulty with swallowing.

Treatment of stroke

Probably 50–75 per cent of stroke episodes result in admission to hospital, mainly because the victim is too helpless to be looked after at home. Intensive nursing will be needed for the unconscious patient. A brain scan is occasionally required to clarify the precise nature of the stroke. If there is difficulty with swallowing persisting after recovery of consciousness, giving fluids intravenously is sufficient for a few days but the insertion of a stomach tube to provide nourishment occasionally becomes necessary. There is at present no clear-cut, immediate treatment to limit the loss of brain cells, although there is some promising research in progress.

As soon as the patient has recovered consciousness the next, critical phase of treatment commences—rehabilitation by family, nurses, speech therapist, physiotherapist, and occupational therapist. This will involve a long and hard battle. In general, muscle power recovers almost as much as it is ever going to within three months, but a recovery of a further ten per cent or so continues throughout a whole year.

Outcome

Stroke is generally an indication of widespread arterial disease, and although there is a considerable risk of recurrence, it is even commoner for survivors to die of coronary disease. On the whole, legs do better than arms, but quality as well as quantity of life is likely to remain restricted (see Table 12.2). Many survivors of major strokes remain very dependent and maintain a miserable existence for months or even years. Those who make a really good recovery and who feel able to resume driving, need to inform the DVLC (in the UK) who will probably instruct them to wait for at least three months and who may then require further information and reports.

Table 12.2   Outcome of stroke survivors (community surveys).

	Percentage
Full or almost full function	25–50
Able to return to work (of those working before)	29–36
Unable to walk outdoors	41
Unable to walk without assistance	20–27
Of those who walk, require an aid	66
Dependent in some aspect of self-care	31–52
Long-term institution	12–21

Source: R. Langton-Hewer (1984). Recovery from stroke. In *Advanced geriatric medicine 4* (ed. J. Grimley Evans and F. I. Caird). Pitman Publishing, London.

Parkinson's disease

Parkinson's disease is another scourge of late life which is much feared, with considerable justification, by elderly people. It is rare in people aged under 50 but affects about 1.5 per cent of the population over 60. It develops extremely insidiously, quite unlike a stroke, and the patient may conclude that he or she is slowing up, simply 'due to age'. One of the main features is shaking of the hands, arms, legs, and occasionally jaw, tongue, head, and even trunk, which often starts asymmetrically and comes on when sitting idly, is at its worst in front of other people, is improved by purposeful activity, and disappears during sleep. This tremor gives the game away, but it can be confused with other types of tremor, and anyway is not invariably present. The other principal features are much less obvious and comprise stiffness and slowness of movement. These lead on to an unstable, shuffling gait, and falls; and to an unblinking, expressionless face, a feeble voice, drooling, impaired handwriting, constipation, and muscle weakness and pain.

The cause of Parkinson's disease

This is one of those mysterious diseases of the brain, like Alzheimer's disease, in which a group of cells dies off causing a loss of vital neurotransmitters, in this case dopamine, and by the time the disease appears there has probably been an 80 per cent reduction. Why the cells die is unknown and it seems to have very little to do with heredity. Sometimes the action of dopamine is blocked by other drugs, notably tranquillizers, and occasionally toxic substances or repeated trauma cause the disease in younger people, but the viral encephalitis that caused a large number of cases earlier this century is no longer prevalent.

Treatment

Treatment is often very effective. Physiotherapy can be extremely helpful, but when the patient is handicapped it is usual also to give a drug which increases brain dopamine levels. These include levodopa which is converted into dopamine, and selegeline, which enhances the quantity available. Other agents act as dopamine supporters. Perhaps two thirds of patients make a good response. Speech therapy can also be effective. Unfortunately it remains true that the illness is progressive and perhaps after five years or so one is likely to run into trouble. Much research is being done on Parkinson's disease, including work on the ethical minefield of fetal brain cell transplantation. These cells do not provoke the rejection reaction that adult tissue causes, and they can settle in and thrive in their new environment: encouraging results have been reported from Sweden, but research is still at an early stage.

Motor neurone disease

This is a progressive disorder of the nerve cells which supply the muscles, which becomes most common after the age of 50 (unlike multiple sclerosis, which most often comes on between the ages of 20 and 40). The affected muscles 'melt away' and can sometimes be seen to quiver under the skin. Any muscles may be affected but those of the legs, hands, tongue, and throat are most vulnerable. The condition is not severely painful and mental function remains intact; bladder and bowel are under perfect control. If only the legs are affected, the disease may progress for many years with little limitation of the quantity or quality of life; when the muscles of swallowing are involved (progressive bulbar palsy), the course of the disease is usually rapid and death soon occurs—usually due to pneumonia, as food spills over into the lungs and causes irritation and infection.

Unfortunately the cause of this condition is unknown and there are currently no effective methods of treatment.

13   Mobility

The ability to walk freely and safely is something that most of us take for granted. Like most of the good things in life our ability to walk without effort and thought is only appreciated when threatened or lost.

The 1988 survey by the Office of Population Censuses and Surveys on disability in the UK showed just how often this facility is impaired. Locomotor problems represented the most frequent disability and affected over 4 million people. Three quarters of those thus affected were aged over 75 years, which means that about one half of people over 75 have some difficulty with movement. This may range from discomfort on climbing stairs for many, to being totally bed-ridden for a few. Disability not only becomes more common with increasing age, it is also likely to become more severe.

However, modern medicine and surgery have developed techniques and treatments which can modify, reverse, or control many of the pathologies that can impair walking. Even irreversible problems can be eased by the use of technical advances to overcome the handicaps that may result. It is therefore important to remain optimistic and determined, even in the face of apparently severe threats to mobility. With the right attitudes and help, an independent lifestyle need not be lost (see Table 13.1).

Causes of immobility

Arthritis is by far and away the most common cause of difficulty in walking and is covered in this chapter. Some other causes are listed below:

Strokes

Parkinson's disease

Motor neurone disease

Tiredness

Breathlessness

Dizziness

Faintness

Heart failure

Painful feet.

Other neurological conditions are covered in Chapter 11.

Table 13.1   The management of arthritis.

1. Attitude	— remain optimistic and determined to retain mobility: 'use it or lose it'
2. Seek advice	— from doctor
3. Physiotherapy	— to strengthen surrounding and supporting muscles
4. Aids	— to redistribute body weight, e.g. a walking stick or frame
5. Adaptations	— to the environment, e.g. chair at correct height
6. Drug treatment	— simple analgesics to control pain, e.g. paracetamol (Panadol): anti-inflammatory drugs to control the destructive process e.g. Brufen.
7. Surgery	— e.g. to replace damaged joints
8. Alternative forms of mobility	— e.g. wheelchairs

Arthritis

By the time we reach old age most of us will have some evidence of osteoarthritis in some of our major joints. The cause of this condition (in common with most forms of arthritis) is unknown. There is, however, no doubt that the recurrent trauma to the joints plays an important role in causation. This probably accounts for the increasing incidence with increasing age—reflecting the unavoidable damage that is inflicted on our joints during a long and active life. People who have exposed individual joints to particularly excessive wear and tear throughout life are the most likely to develop the pathological changes of osteoarthritis. Essentially the condition is due to the destruction of the cartilage layer which covers the ends of the bones at the joints. Without this covering, the friction which occurs with each movement increases—the joint becomes less efficient and movement becomes painful and some-times audible. Because of decreased use of the joint, its surrounding muscles become weaker and are less able to move and support the joint. In the late stages, deformity occurs and the surrounding muscles become stiff and fibrotic hence hindering normal function even more.

Hips and knees are commonly involved and when painful this affects walking, whilst shoulder involvement affects many activities of daily living. The spine is also frequently affected. In the early stages of the disorder pain-relieving tablets enable continued use of the joints. Extra strengthening may be gained by activity or specific exercises—the special skills of a physiotherapist will be invaluable in planning such courses of treatment. If the joint changes progress to such an extent that normal activities become painful, then referral to an orthopaedic surgeon is needed for consideration of joint replacement. Combined metal and plastic joints inserted into the hip have been one of the most successful developments of modern surgery and have truly prolonged active life for many patients. Unfortunately the new joints do not last as long as nature's originals and a further replacement may be needed after ten or so years of use.

Rheumatoid arthritis

Rheumatoid arthritis is less common but it maybe more severe and has a tendency to be more crippling than other forms of arthritic pathology. It can affect any joint, but involvement of the joints of the arms and hands make it very effective in stripping a patient of his independence. In this condition the joint-lining membrane goes berserk and rapidly overgrows, extending into and eroding the surrounding cartilage and bone. The disease may arise at any time of life, from childhood to old age. However, the elderly will account for many cases as there are by this stage in life those who have struggled with the disease for many years as well as new cases arising in old age. Initial treatment concentrates on suppressing pain. Physiotherapy will attempt to preserve maximum function. More potent forms of medication, such as steroids, gold, and penicillamine, are used in severe forms only, as the side-effects of these preparations can be severe. In some cases, surgical intervention may be required.

Gout

Of all the arthritic conditions, this traditionally is most associated with ageing. The caricature of the debauched old man with an excessively painful foot, enlarged big toe, and short temper is well known. However, frugal living will not automatically protect from this very painful disorder. The joints become painful because of inflammation caused in the joint cavity by the precipitation of small crystals of uric acid. There is an accumulation of uric acid in the body and its synthesis is reduced by an enzyme-inhibiting drug known as allopurinol (Zyloric).

Pseudo-gout is a very similar condition: again, crystals form in the joints, but the mechanism is entirely unknown. The only treatment available is therefore that of symptomatic relief, so pain-killers with anti-inflammatory properties are used to suppress symptoms.

Falls

Falls are unpleasant and dangerous and unfortunately become more common with increasing age (Table 13.2). Throughout life, women are more unsteady than men. The situation worsens at the time of

Table 13.2 Estimated incidence of falls in one year

Age-groups	Women	Men
65–69	1 in 3	1 in 7
80–84	1 in 2	1 in 3

menopause—but the inequality between the sexes begins to disappear in advanced old age. Those who are most frail and disabled are those at greatest risk. This is illustrated by the fact that falls in institutions are much more common than falls at home. The circumstances of falls also differ. At home, falls are most likely to occur in the living room or on the stairs. In hospitals and care homes they seem to happen most often when rising from a chair, bed, or toilet.

An increasing frequency of falls is a bad prognostic sign and indicates serious underlying health problems. Almost 50 per cent of frequent fallers who are suffering from another illness will be dead within a six-month period. Their deaths, however, will be due to the underlying illnesses rather than to any injury sustained during a fall. Nevertheless, falling itself is dangerous and up to 4000 pensioners in the UK die each year as a consequence of falling. Many more suffer pain and anxiety which further restricts their mobility as a consequence of falling.

The causes of falling are legion, but a clear description of the sequence of events will be of great help to the doctor when it comes to deciding on the reasons and the subsequent treatment. It is usually possible to categorize episodes into one of two types—trips and 'turns'.

Trips

These are episodes which can usually be explained away. The faller will realize with hindsight that with greater care the accident could have been avoided. Trips are most likely to happen to reasonably mobile people—they are usually due to either carelessness, clumsiness, or known disability, or are secondary to environmental factors. Some of the disabilities which may lead to falls are:

(1) arthritis and rheumatism;

(2) stroke;

(3) Parkinson's disease;

(4) peripheral neuropathy (numbness of feet);

(5) ear disease—deafness, tinnitus, and loss of balance;

(6) visual impairment.

Disabled people should therefore take great care, especially when changing their position (for instance, rising from sitting) or when changing direction, for example, on turning. Remember that some drugs, such as sleeping tablets and alcohol, will increase the liability to fall in vulnerable people and their use should therefore be avoided or restricted.

Environmental hazards such as trailing flexes, abandoned articles on the floor, loose rugs, and poorly lit stairs and steps are a risk to all. The risks become even greater when associated with poor vision (for example, cataracts) or impaired gait (for example in Parkinson's disease or arthritis) or impaired balance.

'Turns'

These are more frightening than trips because they cannot usually be explained away by the victim. They are also more likely to be associated with a change in consciousness, may happen at any time, and the patient will feel powerless to control the episodes. They are symptoms of underlying problems, usually heart or brain disease. Sudden changes in heart-rate or rhythm may lead to a fall; the experience of palpitations may act as a clue to the cause. If the mechanism can be identified then prevention may be available through drug treatment or the insertion of a cardiac pacemaker (see Chaper 16). Sudden changes in blood pressure may lead to falls—these may also be secondary to changes in heart-rate but also to the side-effects of drugs. Sudden changes in brain function, as in epilepsy, may lead to blackouts and falls, and this can develop in late life. Reversible and transient changes in the blood supply, both in quality (such as reduced sugar levels) or quantity may also lead to fits or small transient strokes. In some cases, after examination and investigation, it will be possible to offer protection from further episodes—so help should be sought.

The dangers of falls

1. Injury—fracture and bruising.

2. Loss of confidence.

3. Complications of a long lie—hypothermia, pneumonia, pressure-sores.

4. Loss of independence—anxiety in both the victim and carers leading to institutional care.

What to do if you suffer from falls

1. Seek medical help, they may be preventable and controllable.

2. Make your environment as safe and convenient as possible.

3. Reduce the risks of a long lie, for example:
   - (i) learn how to get up from the floor by rolling, crawling, and climbing up furniture—a physiotherapist will advise;
   - (ii) keep warm and comfortable if unable to rise by keeping blankets and pillows in an accessible place, for instance on the floor;
   - (iii) invest in an alarm system, preferably a body-worn personal alarm tuned into a warden system;
   - (iv) encourage frequent callers so that you will soon be discovered if an accident occurs.

If you cannot be protected from your falls and you wish to continue living in your own home you owe it to yourself and to those who care about you to ensure that the risks to which you are exposed are kept to a minimum. Remember that a move to a care home will not abolish falls secondary to illness—but more and earlier help will be available to assist you after a fall.

Fractures

Three types of fractures are common in old age. The vulnerable sites are the wrists, the hip, and the vertebral bodies of the spine. The peak age of the incidence of each varies site by site, but in all instances women are more seriously affected than men—usually by a factor of five or six (see Figs 13.1 and 13.2).

Wrist fractures are most common at the time of the menopause. It is at this time that women can become more unsteady—but of course continue to lead active lives and wear unsuitable shoes. They normally try to save themselves when falling by putting out an outstretched hand and thus exposing the wrist to damage. As this protective mechanism declines with increasing age and frailty, the incidence of wrist fracture falls, but that of hip trauma increases.

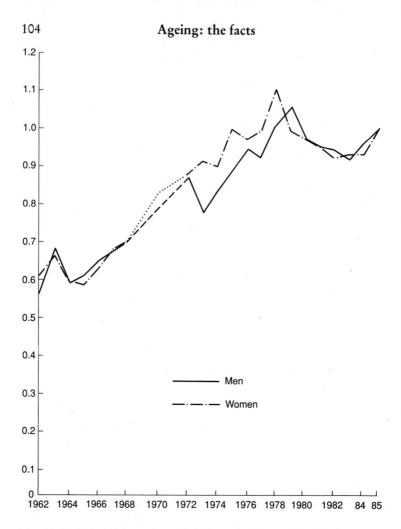

Fig. 13.1 Hospital in-patient admissions for fractured neck of femur in men and women over 65 years of age.
Source: HIPE and OPCS.

Hip fractures are important, not only because of the pain and discomfort that they cause, but also because they have an adverse effect on lifespan and independence. Many frail, elderly patients fail to survive their fracture (about 3000 each year) and those that do survive may have a reduced life expectancy. Although surgical

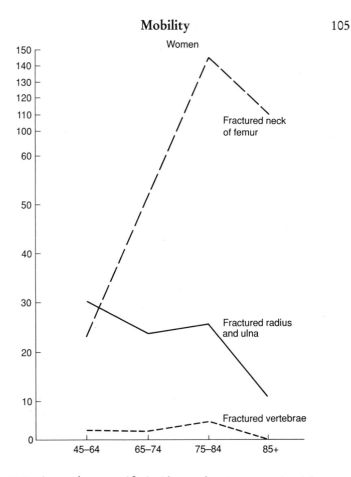

Fig. 13.2 Age and sex-specific incidence of various age-related fractures in women.
Source: HIPE.

techniques of repair have been revolutionized, about half the survivors will have a reduced level of independence after sustaining a fracture. The cost of treatment to the health service is also considerable, even though savings have been made by drastically increasing the speed of recovery and reducing the length of hospital stay. The estimated cost to the NHS in 1988 for fractured neck of femur was £160 million and this is probably a significant underestimate.

Fractures of spinal vertebrae cause pain, loss of height, and curvature of the spine (sometimes known as a dowager's hump).

Why do old bones break?

The simple reason is because of the combination of more frequent falls in old age and the increased fragility of ageing bones. However, the rise in incidence in fractures is greater than can be explained on demographic evidence alone. It would therefore seem that something is unusual about the bones of the current generation of elderly women.

Osteoporosis

This is the name for the thinning of bones which occurs after the age of 30 years. In both men and women bone mass reduces with age (see Fig 13.3). This decline accelerates in women at the time of

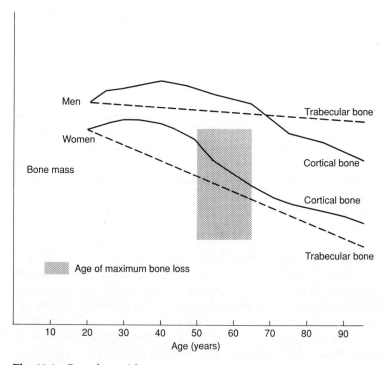

Fig. 13.3 Bone loss with age.

the menopause. In addition, women achieve a smaller maximum bone mass at age 30 and then go on to lose bone for a longer period because of their increased longevity over men. Hence the extra risk of fracture to which women are exposed. Many risk factors have been identified in the causation of osteoporosis, including the following:

- Ageing
- Female sex
- Premature or artificial menopause
- Multiple pregnancies
- Family history of osteoporosis and fracture
- Ethnic background—black people are better protected
- Body build—slim, fair women most at risk
- Lack of exercise
- Calcium deficient diet
- Smoking
- Alcohol
- Medical treatment, especially steroids and gastric surgery
- Other medical conditions, for example overactive thyroid and adrenal glands.

Protection from osteoporosis

A lifelong strategy is required, involving the adoption of a healthy lifestyle; a balanced diet of natural foods, exercise, and the avoidance of detrimental habits, such as smoking and the drinking of alcohol. In this way the maximum bone mass may be initially built up before the age of 30 and then maintained. A threat to bone which can be modified is that caused by the menopause. There is good evidence that hormone replacement therapy (HRT) can prevent the sudden acceleration in bone loss that affects some women. Monthly treatment with oestrogen will slow the natural bone changes. Oestrogen will also offer some protection to some women against heart attacks and will improve the condition of their skin and hair, as well as relieving menopausal symptoms. However, there are potential risks—particularly of cancer of the womb. By supplementing the treatment with progesterone this complication may usually be avoided but there may be a small increased risk of breast cancer. There are several other disadvantages of HRT such as the continued inconvenience of menstrual blood loss and the

uncertainty of how long treatment should be undertaken. Most
people would however suggest a course of about ten years, i.e. until
the age of about 65 years. It should be realized that HRT cannot
replace bone already lost, but can only slow down the loss. Not all
women are at equal risk and some selection is therefore needed for
those with multiple risk factors.

Bone density can be measured by expensive and non-invasive
techniques such as densitometry, and those demonstrating an
abnormally rapid bone loss should receive HRT. Unfortunately
this investigation is not routinely available through the NHS, but
tests can sometimes be arranged through private clinics.

Other conditions causing bone fragility

Paget's disease

This is due to areas of hyperactivity in bones. The bones become
distorted and are sometimes painful. Although enlarged, the bones
are more fragile than normal. If symptoms are troublesome (and
many cases are asymptomatic) then relief can be obtained by the
use of analgesics and special hormone injections (calcitonin).
Although the condition is common—there are about three-quarters
of a million cases in the UK alone—the cause is unknown, although
there are pointers that suggest a viral infection.

Osteomalacia

This is a softening of bone due to its impaired production. The
underlying cause is a lack of vitamin D. This deficiency may result
from a poor diet (oily fish and dairy products are good sources of
vitamin D) or poor absorption resulting from bowel disease or lack
of exposure to sunlight. The latter is the most important as most
people produce their own vitamin D in their skin when it is exposed
to sunshine. When the condition occurs in children it is known as
rickets—but elderly people are also vulnerable to the same bone
condition. The resulting soft bones have an increased liability to
fracture. The condition is corrected by giving extra supplies of
vitamin D.

Cancer in bones

Areas of bone may be weakened because of cancerous changes.
These may arise directly in the bones or occur as a cancer spreads

from another source, such as the prostate, breast, or lung. Although these lesions are usually painful this is not always the case and they may only come to light when a fracture occurs through an area of weakened bone. At this stage there may still be no evidence of the primary growth. Painful areas of bone can be improved by giving a course of X-ray treatment and some cases will also benefit from special hormone treatment—depending on the nature of the problem.

Transport

Driving

The accident rate increases after the age of 60 (Fig. 13.4). Activities such as turning across the stream of oncoming traffic and pulling away from the kerb become increasingly dangerous—probably due

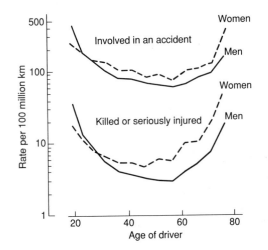

Fig. 13.4 Rates of accidents and serious injury or death in car drivers by age and sex (Great Britain 1986).

to the driver's lack of awareness of other road users. It therefore becomes more important that elderly drivers concentrate on their driving and pay attention to the road and other vehicles. Distractions such as in-car entertainment and conversations with passengers should be avoided. Driving is best restricted to off-peak times and when natural light is available. Journeys should be well-planned in advance and should be looked upon as an experience to be enjoyed. The rush should be taken out of journeys and regular rest and refreshment stops should be included to make the journey both more enjoyable and also safer. For really long expeditions many days should be taken for their completion.

A current UK driving licence is valid until the age of 70 years. After that birthday a declaration of good health has to be made every three years. If a driver's health becomes impaired, then the licensing authority should be informed and its advice sought. Temporary cessation of driving is necessary after some acute illnesses, such as a heart attack. The onset of conditions which are characterized by sudden and unexpected episodes of altered consciousness, such as epilepsy, cardiac irregularities, and minor strokes prohibit further driving. Similarly, driving is excluded by significantly impaired vision, loss of dexterity as in severe arthritis, stroke damage, or Parkinson's disease. In some instances modification to the car may allow a person to continue to drive. The Association of Advanced Motorists is willing to test drivers who are anxious about their ability to continue to drive safely.

Public transport

When driving has ceased, as a result of frailty and disability, the alternative methods of transport are limited. Public transport will present many problems because of its inaccessibility, including both walking to the bus stop and standing to wait. In addition, climbing the step to mount the bus may become impossible, and standing and moving about on a moving vehicle may become dangerous. Buses can be modified to overcome some of these obstacles, but special vehicles are rarely available.

Social transport schemes are run by some local authorities in the UK. Where available, it is possible to request a subsidized car— often driven by a volunteer. Such schemes can only offer help when it is impossible to use public transport for the same journey. Some cars can be modified so that entry is made easier for a disabled passenger and some taxis can take wheelchairs if a portable ramp is available to ensure the chair can be pushed into the taxi and locked into position. The disabled person can then be safely transported in his own wheelchair.

When driving has to be abandoned it may be cheaper to pay for taxis rather than have the continued upkeep of a rarely used car. In some areas the local authority provides subsidies for taxi services for disabled people.

Mobility allowances can only be claimed when disability occurs before pensionable age. Problems that occur after that age do not make a person eligible for such financial help. This is an example of legislation ageism.

Flying

Many elderly people wish to fly either for holiday reasons or to visit distant relatives. In a well-pressurized aircraft there is unlikely to be any problem. However patients with severe anaemia and severe chest and heart conditions may encounter difficulties. The important precaution is to discuss the matter with the airline well in advance of the proposed journey. With an adequate early warning most companies can make appropriate arrangements. Moving about the airport is often more likely to present problems than the time spent in the air, although most airlines now supply wheelchairs and arrange accelerated passage through departure procedures and escort right to the plane, including access by lift if necessary. It should be remembered that cabin crew are not medically trained (apart from first aid) and they are not allowed to give help with personal hygiene as they are primarily 'food handlers'. If help with personal care is needed you will have to provide your own escort. If extra space is needed, then extra charges may be made to compensate for the loss of seats. Special diets can be provided if ordered in advance.

Patients should not fly within two weeks of a chest or abdominal operation as complications may arise. After a heart attack, flying should be delayed for at least three weeks. Regular medication should continue to be taken as normal, especially drugs such as anticonvulsants as the risk of fits may be increased.

During the flight, alcohol should be avoided but fluids should be taken in plentiful amounts. Regular movement of limbs is advised, especially on long flights, to avoid stiffness of joints and thrombosis of the leg veins. If it can be afforded, first class travel offers more opportunities for movement.

14 Nutrition and digestion

Diet

There is much concern about the eating habits of the elderly. However, there is good evidence that healthy old people eat as well as the rest of the population. Their total intake tends to be lower but matches their reduced physical activity. Their preferences are also different from those of the younger generation but their diet is generally well balanced. The situation is only likely to change at times of stress, such as bereavement and illness, or in people of eccentric habits.

Nevertheless, there is a constant demand for advice about suitable dietary measures in old age. Because of wide individual variations and preferences, it is only possible to give guidelines.

It becomes increasingly important that excess weight should not be carried as degenerative changes in joints and the heart may mean that these begin to feel the strain. Those who are overweight must therefore try even harder than before to reduce their weight. Avoidance of fat and highly refined carbohydrate (such as sugar) is the best way of achieving weight reduction. Bulk (to avoid feelings of hunger and to provide bowel residue) is best taken by increasing the amount of fibre in the diet—converting to wholemeal bread, flour, pasta, whole-grain rice, and bran-based cereals. Fresh vegetables (including potatoes) and fruit provide both fibre and vitamins.

A balanced diet

Recommended ingredients for a balanced daily diet would include:

1. one pint (500 ml) milk, skimmed if obesity is a problem;

2. one item of fresh fruit daily;

3. one egg daily, or one portion of meat, fish, or cheese;

4. one portion of fresh vegetables.

These items can be used in any way; for example milk for drinking or cooking. Similarly the egg may be used in cooking or eaten on its own. Additional foods should also be taken and the above list is just a recommended minimum. It is useful to remember that some commonplace foods are fortified with vitamins, for example vitamin C in dehydrated potatoes, and vitamin D in margarine. Frozen foods have the same nutrient values as fresh, but overcooking always destroys the vitamins. Prepared foods tend to deteriorate with storing, except when frozen. Many of the items on the recommended list may be available on the doorstep from the milkman (he may also carry fresh fruit juice, a good source of vitamin C). It is important that a stock of emergency rations—for example, frozen, dried, and tinned foods—should be kept. These may be needed if bad weather conditions, transport failure, or illness make it impossible to get out to the shops.

People who enjoy good health usually enjoy their food. Failure of appetite may well be an indication that something is wrong and a doctor should be consulted.

Special dietary problems and needs are likely to arise in times of ill-health. During a brief illness, the first essential is the maintenance of a good fluid intake, as the normal thirst mechanism seems to be reduced in the elderly and dehydration is likely to occur. But so long as small and frequent drinks are taken, the complications of dehydration can be avoided. The drinks should preferably contain some calorific value, the addition of glucose being the simplest method. In a more prolonged illness it is necessary to add further nutrients to such a liquid diet. Commercially prepared compounds such as Complan are readily available, and a mixture of milk, eggs, and sugar also provide a nutritious liquid diet.

On these modified diets, attention must be paid to the patient's bowels. When only fluids are taken there is a risk of constipation; and feeds thickened with dairy products and sugars can cause diarrhoea. The ill patient is likely to find the usual bulking foods unacceptable, and Fybogel, Celevac, or Isogel may provide easier alternatives.

Specific illnesses require special diets and advice from a dietitian is needed. Diabetics, for example, must have a controlled amount of carbohydrate and a limited fat intake. Patients with renal failure should have their protein intake restricted. In cases of pancreatic disease, a low-fat diet is desirable. In wasting, malignant disease and chronic infections, extra protein supplements are beneficial. In all cases, attractively presented food and the provision of favourite dishes is the most pleasant way of encouraging a flagging appetite.

Food safety

Over recent years in the United Kingdom there has been a steadily rising incidence of food-borne infection. Problems with salmonella, campylobacter, and listeria have been most marked. Elderly people are particularly vulnerable for the following reasons.

1. Outbreaks often arise from institutionally prepared foods, for example in hospitals and care homes and day centres which may also prepare meals on wheels.

2. Food handling, preparation, and storage may be difficult for disabled elderly people living at home, and standards may fall as a result.

3. Frail, elderly people have a lower resistance to infection.

4. The consequence of infection are more likely to be severe in vulnerable elderly people.

5. Reluctance to waste means that leftovers are saved and kept to be eaten at a later date in order to be economical.

In order to avoid unnecessary risks, the following guidelines are recommended.

1. Avoid eating uncooked food known to carry the risk of bacterial contamination, such as eggs (salmonella), soft cheeses (listeria), and also pâtés.

2. Ensure that food is stored at a safe, low temperature, i.e. less than 4 °C. Check that your fridge and freezer work properly and that their doors shut tightly.

3. Follow the makers' instructions, for example with prepared meals when using a microwave.

4. Respect recommended dates and ensure that frozen foods are properly defrosted before cooking.

5. If in doubt, always overcook.

6. Do not save and reheat previously prepared meals, such as meals on wheels or food prepared by neighbours. Eat what you can when it is provided and discard any remainders.

Digestion

Intermittent symptoms from the digestive system are common throughout life, and are generally not of great significance. The magnitude of the inconvenience is not matched by serious consequences. However, during the ageing process abnormalities of the gut become increasingly frequent, and symptoms may therefore change and increase in importance. Perversely, some potentially dangerous abdominal conditions sometimes become asymptomatic in older people. In additional some bowel upsets are due to changes in other distant systems. Diagnostic problems in digestive upsets, therefore, become increasingly complex with ageing.

Loss of appetite and weight

Persistent loss of appetite and sudden weight loss must always be taken seriously. Usually they are non-specific markers of an underlying illness. Chronic ill-health due to longstanding heart failure, recurrent bronchitis, or severe arthritis and many other conditions may be responsible. An occult growth or infection in any system can lead to weight loss. An upset in the endocrine glands, as for example in diabetes, or an over-active thyroid gland, can lead to dramatic weight reduction, but these are not usually associated with a poor appetite. The opposite may even be the case.

Psychological disturbances—especially depression—can also significantly upset a patient's desire for food and the resultant reduced intake can lead to weight loss. Many medications can also impair appetite and cause nausea and vomiting.

Because weight loss and appetite changes are such ubiquitous complaints, it is the associated symptoms that act as clues to the site of the precipitating cause. Nausea, vomiting, abdominal pain, and changes in bowel habit are all concurrent problems that may indicate a potential gastrointestinal abnormality.

Nausea and vomiting

Nausea and vomiting are not exclusive to disorders of the digestive system. They can also occur in some neurological conditions, especially where the inner ear and its balance functions are impaired, or where pressure inside the skull becomes raised. Endogenous poisoning due to the accumulation of excess waste products, such as occurs in kidney failure, may also be responsible.

When some of the symptoms are caused by disorders in the gastrointestinal tract, the precipitating abnormality will usually be found in the upper part, such as the oesophagus (gullet), stomach, duodenum, or gallbladder and its ducts.

In the oesophagus the two most likely problems are obstruction and irritation. When obstruction occurs, food becomes difficult to swallow, and can be felt to stick behind the breastbone, and may be regurgitated or vomited. When irritation is the main problem, the vomiting is likely to be associated with pain—particularly heartburn, where acid can be felt rising up into the throat. This sensation is, in fact, usually due to acid being allowed to rise up out of the stomach and hence irritate the sensitive lining of the gullet. A defect at the junction of the oesophagus and stomach is the usual cause and this is called a hiatus hernia.

Both of these symptom complexes—regurgitation and food that sticks, and vomiting with heartburn—normally need to be investigated. The technique used in the first instance is a barium swallow, where in this test the patient swallows a radio-opaque substance and its progress down the gullet can be observed on X-rays. Thus the site of the abnormality can nearly always be identified without difficulty, although there may be problems in establishing its nature for certain. Where there is doubt it will be necessary to arrange for the lesion to be seen directly; this can be done by the use of a narrow, flexible telescope (fibrotic endoscope), and even more usefully a small piece can be removed by the instrument. Close microscopic examination can then be undertaken and the precise nature of the problem determined. This course of action is necessary when it is feared that an obstructing lesion is due to a cancerous growth. When such a serious diagnosis has been confirmed, its treatment will depend on the exact site and extent of the growth, the choice lying between radiotherapy to shrink the growth, its removal by surgery, or a bypass by a surgically inserted tube. Simple, benign obstructions can sometimes be easily stretched—although this procedure may need to be repeated at regular intervals.

A hiatus hernia is an inconvenient defect but rarely serious, and surgical intervention to correct it is rarely required. Much symptomatic improvement can be obtained by simple measures such as weight loss—where there is obesity—avoidance of stooping and straining, and the regular use of preparations to neutralize or reduce acid secretions. A hiatus hernia is found in about 60 per cent of all people over the age of 60 years, and most of these (three-quarters) do get some symptoms (usually heartburn).

Indigestion

Indigestion implies pain or discomfort associated with eating. It is a very vague but common symptom. Throughout life, about one-third of people experience such problems, and in old age it rises to over a half. Most people become familiar with their own particular problems and they adapt their diet and lifestyle to minimize their distress, while maximizing their pleasures. Only if their symptoms change in nature or severity are they likely to seek medical help. The most common cause of indigestion in late life is a hiatus hernia (see above).

Peptic ulceration and malignancy

Peptic ulceration of the stomach or duodenum is the next most frequent cause of indigestion (see Fig 14.1). In both condition, the lining of the stomach or duodenum will have become eroded, either because of excess acid activity or because of reduced resistance of the lining to normal wear and tear. Elderly people are particularly vulnerable to complications such as bleeding and perforation.

Another increased risk in elderly patients is that the stomach lesion may be malignant. Confirmation of this possibility is clearly important but may be difficult. There are unlikely to be any clear indications from the patient's symptoms—the barium meal X-ray may be inconclusive. The most reliable method of investigation is gastroscopy, where the stomach is inspected with a flexible fibroptic instrument. This can normally be performed in an out-patient clinic and a piece of the ulcer can be removed for detailed examination. It is only complicated ulcers which necessitate an operation. The majority respond well to treatment with medicines and tablets, especially cimetidine, ranitidine, and omeprazole. Aggravating factors such as smoking, drinking alcohol, or taking aspirin and similar drugs, should be avoided. Although these ulcers tend to run a fluctuating course, they should not seriously interfere with the pursuit of a full and enjoyable life.

Gallstones

Gallstones are another cause of indigestion, which increases in frequency on ageing (Fig. 14.1). The incidence reaches 30 per cent in women and 25 per cent in men, but in many cases they do not cause symptoms. Sharp pains on the right side of the abdomen below the ribs is the most common way in which gallstones can advertise their presence, and these pains may become very severe and require painkillers. The constant irritation by the stone may cause the gallbladder to become inflamed and tender. The stone may escape from the gallbladder but lodge in the duct on its way into the bowel. As well as being painful, this may also lead to jaundice as the main exit from the liver may become blocked. The patient's skin becomes increasingly yellow if the blockage persists. The correct diagnosis may be made on X-ray examination (cholecystogram) or ultrasound techniques (using reflections of sound waves to reveal the stones). When symptoms are severe there is no alternative to surgical removal of the stones. The recent development of 'keyhole' surgery makes this a less formidable event. Painless jaundice may occur as a side-effect of some drugs (tranquillizers) and secondary to pancreatic cancer.

Constipation

Many elderly people worry unnecessarily about their bowels. It should be appreciated that not everybody has their bowels open each day—the actual frequency of bowel clearance is not important, but regularity is. For some people it is normal for their bowels to move only on every third day, and for others on alternate days or a similar pattern. There should only be concern if the pattern changes or the motions become difficult to pass. Small hard motions are the most difficult to evacuate. Poor dietary habits are the most frequent cause of constipation, and the simplest method of correction is to increase the amount of fibrous bulk in the food; fruit, vegetables

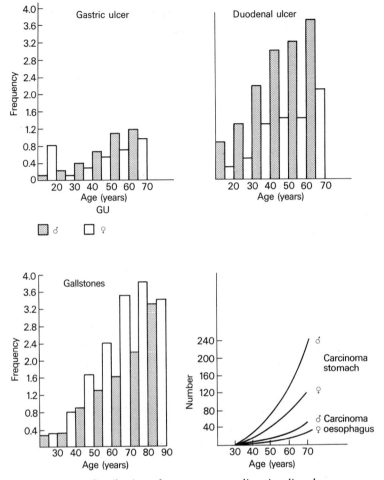

Fig. 14.1 Age distribution of some common digestive disorders.

(especially beans), and bran and wholemeal bread and flour are items in the diet which need to be increased.

Causes

Constipation can occur as a side-effect of many drugs. Analgesics (especially codeine derivatives), antidepressants and the older anti-parkinsonian drugs are particularly guilty. The abuse of violent purgatives during a long life can leave the bowel exhausted, flabby, and unable to work properly. Imbalance of the body's chemistry and glands can also lead to constipation. High calcium levels due to hyperactivity of the parathyroid gland is a rare but significant cause. Underactivity of the thyroid gland (myxoedema) is a more common cause of constipation but once identified is easily corrected.

Constipation can be an early presenting symptom of obstruction of the lower bowel. It is for this reason that it must be taken seriously if it arises as a new symptom in later life. The necessary investigations (sigmoidoscopy and barium enema examinations) are simple and the surgical removal of an obstructing growth will be successful if no unnecessary delay has been allowed to occur.

Laxatives

If help is required to ensure comfortable bowel evacuation, a natural form of assistance is preferable. Simply increasing the bulk of the stools is often sufficient to resolve the problem of constipation, and this may be achieved by taking a diet with increased amount of fibre (such as bran, wholemeal bread, extra fruit and vegetables). Bulking preparations are also available—Celevac, Isogel, Fybogel, and Lactulose—which act by absorbing water when in the large bowel and thus increase the amount of residue to be excreted.

Stool softeners—such as dioctyl and Normax are also safe and effective; the latter also contains a small amount of gut stimulant. Preparations containing irritants such as phenolphthalein are best avoided, and lubricating substances such as liquid paraffin also have many undesirable side-effects so cannot be recommended.

Mild stimulating preparations such as senna and lubricants like milpar are also commonly used.

Diarrhoea

An isolated episode of loose motions is no more significant in old age than in earlier life. It is only in infants and small children that serious sequelae are likely to arise. A brief, self-limiting infection is usually found to be the cause. Simple measures concerning personal hygiene and a light liquid diet are all that are required to enable the bowel to make a spontaneous recovery.

Chronic inflammatory conditions are the most likely cause of prolonged diarrhoea in older people. The most common is diverticular disease, where pouches arising from the large bowel become inflamed and irritated, pain and diarrhoea are then likely to occur. These pouches occur in the majority of the elderly in the western world, and probably result from excess pressures in the bowel generated by the force needed to expel small, hard motions. Improving the consistency of the stools is the best method of treatment and prevention.

Inflammatory conditions, such as Crohn's disease and ulcerative colitis, are usually associated with younger patients, but both illnesses can also occur in elderly people. Impaired bowel function due to reduction in its blood supply is another cause of diarrhoea, and one almost exclusive to the elderly. Episodes of diarrhoea and abdominal pain are most likely to occur after eating, and the patient will have difficulty in maintaining his normal weight.

Activity at the upper end of the gut may also result in diarrhoea, dietary excesses of unaccustomed food and alcohol being the most common culprits. Medicines are also fairly frequently responsible, especially antibiotics, and excessive doses of digoxin and the abuse of purgatives are other examples. Anxiety can be another potent cause.

Faecal incontinence

Faecal incontinence is a disaster for both the patient and his immediate carers. However, if the patient if aware of the problem it is likely that a treatable cause will be found. If the problem has an incurable cause, it will be least be possible for such a patient to cooperate with his carers so that the inconvenience and distress are minimized. In such circumstances a method of management can be devised which retains some degree of predictability concerning the patient's bowel habits.

The most difficult patients to look after are those who have no insight into their bowel problem, usually due to severe widespread brain damage. Patients with dementia form the largest segment of this group; a few lose their social veneer as a consequence of a tumour situated at the front of the brain. It is at least comforting that patients are usually unaware of the distress and unpleasantness associated with their lack of bowel control. The suffering tends to be entirely on the side of onlookers and helpers. When incontinence takes the form of uncontrolled watery diarrhoea, which is lost almost continuously, it is essential that a search is made for severe constipation. This paradox is difficult for a layman to accept; however, when a patient with reduced powers of awareness becomes very constipated a large, hard stool may be acting as a blockage to the bowel. Motions higher up may then liquify, and ooze past the obstruction to run unhindered from the anus. Removal of the blockage (an unpleasant procedure for all concerned) and correction of the stool consistency help attempts to regain bowel control.

Patients who have persistent faecal incontinence and are aware of their problem are likely to have either a neurological condition affecting the spinal cord, such as severe trauma, a growth, or a degenerative condition. Alternatively they may have a local destructive lesion affecting the normal opening and closing mechanisms of the lower end of the bowel. A growth or gross laxity of the muscles so that the bowel can prolapse or turn inside out are the most likely explanations. Both are easily detected by simply examination and can be corrected by surgical operation.

Transient faecal incontinence

Many transient episodes of incontinence are unfortunate accidents, with the patient literally being caught short. Even fit young people may have such embarrassing accidents if they suffer from an excessively explosive attack of diarrhoea. In older and frailer people the diarrhoea is equally troublesome even when not explosive, particularly when the patient's speed and mobility are hindered by painful arthritis or clumsiness due to a stroke. The awkward combination of loose motions, slow locomotion, and a distant toilet may be more than many disabled people can manage. In these cases attention to their walking and the location of their toilet is as important as consideration of possible causes for the loose motions.

If uncertainty about control remains after proper deliberation has been paid to all aspects of continence, then other methods of management must be contemplated. Special padded pants are available and can avoid much embarrassment and unpleasantness, but they should only be used as a last measure of defence.

Altered bowel habit

This symptom has already been mentioned above in the sections on diarrhoea and constipation. However, its importance justifies repetition. Any persistent alteration in a lifetime's bowel habit merits reporting to the doctor. The change can be the onset of constipation, persistent diarrhoea, or alternation between constipation and looseness of the motions. Any of these symptoms may herald the presence of a serious underlying bowel problem. Early reporting and subsequent investigation will help to identify many problems at a time when curative treatment is still possible.

Although many benign conditions may present in this way, it is also a common and early form of presentation of cancer of the large bowel, and so for this reason must be taken seriously. If the change in bowel habit is also associated with the passage of blood, either fresh bright-red blood or dark altered blood, there is again the risk of an underlying malignant cause—although piles are the most common cause.

15 The bladder and its control

One of the great dreads of ageing is that of loss of bladder control, because of its identification with loss of dignity, and its aesthetically unpleasant associations. Urinary incontinence and mental infirmity are perhaps two of the saddest afflictions that can bedevil old age and which also offer ammunition to those who calumniate it. Incontinence causes considerable distress and suffering to the patient, a great deal of unpleasantness to his carers, and much of the demand for institutional care.

Normal bladder function

The bladder is a muscular reservoir which receives urine formed by the kidneys. Normally it fills without contractions of the muscle until a point is reached when signals are sent conveying the sensation of fullness when the bladder contains perhaps 250 ml of urine. The act of emptying the bladder, or micturition, is a reflex triggered by these sensations arriving at the spinal cord, and consists of the simultaneous contraction of the bladder wall and relaxation of the sphincter mechanism which has been holding the bladder outlet tightly shut. But the sensory messages also travel up the spinal cord to the brain, making us aware of the need to pass urine, and enabling us to send messages back down the cord preventing the reflex from acting until we reach a socially appropriate time and place. Most people will find themselves 'bursting for a pee' when their bladders are holding 400–500 ml of urine. After voiding there should be under 100 ml of urine remaining in the bladder.

What is incontinence?

It is fashionable to think positively in order to avoid accusations of ableism, and continence is easily defined as 'the ability to pass urine in the right place at the right time'. Incontinence, on the other hand, has been described as 'the involuntary loss of urine to a socially or hygienically unacceptable degree', and it has been suggested that what constitutes an unacceptable frequency might be twice a month.

What incontinence is *not*, is the occurrence of 'accidents' due to inability to reach the toilet in time on account of a combination of immobility and poorly situated toilets or strange surroundings. Nor, in a more institutional context, is it making a mess because of fumbling with the bottle.

How common is incontinence?

Epidemiological surveys to indicate the prevalence of a condition yield differing results according to the definition adopted and the population studied. The most consistently incontinent section of the population is, of course, the under-three age group. But this book is concerned with later life, and one commonly quoted survey found that among men aged 15–64, only 1.6 per cent admitted incontinence, whereas over the age of 65 the figure rose to 6.9 per cent. Women are considerably more liable to incontinence than men, and the corresponding figures were 8.5 per cent for the younger ones and 11.6 per cent when aged 65 and over.

What age changes predispose to incontinence?

Firstly, it should be noted that the kidney conveniently arranges to produce more urine during the day than at night, unless a considerable amount of fluid is taken late in the evening. This rhythm is often disturbed as we grow older and getting out of bed to pass urine during the night becomes a regular event. This situation will clearly make nocturnal bed-wetting more likely, especially if the bladder is unstable (see below).

Attention has been drawn to the greater propensity of women to become incontinent, and this is partly due to the inherently less efficient sphincter mechanism related to the shorter female urethra, which also makes the bladder more prone to infection. It may sometimes also result from the damage commonly sustained by the pelvic nerves and musculature during childbirth. The female urogenital tract is also affected by the menopause, when the oestrogen-sensitive lining undergoes degeneration and the function of the urethra deteriorates. In men, a degree of enlargement of the prostate is almost universal in later life (except in those unfortunate enough to have been castrated). Only about 10 per cent of men will require surgery for this.

The bladder in old people tends to become a little shrunken and the walls thicken and become less elastic so that its capacity is somewhat reduced. Finally, and most important of all, it may contract during filling and during the postponement of micturition instead of waiting for permission to void. This is known as instability of the bladder and is extremely common. The contractions are sometimes spontaneous and random, and are sometimes triggered by coughing, standing up, or walking. The characteristic symptom is urgency: the meaning is reasonably self-evident and its presence is betrayed by the instant look of recognition on the patient's face when asked by the doctor, 'Can you hold your urine, or do you need to go at once?' This symptom, in combination with poor mobility and a distant (or occupied) toilet, can readily lead to accidents. Both these changes—the low-capacity, unstable bladder—are more likely if there is other local disease such as marked prostatic enlargement. Spontaneous contractions also occur if there has been damage to the central nervous system so that messages to postpone contraction are either not initiated or fail to get through, and this can happen as a result of strokes, Alzheimer's disease, and other illnesses, A further reason why demented patients are liable to become incontinent is their failure to pass urine prophylactically, for example prior to a concert, a formal dinner, or a shopping expedition: they tend to wait until desperate and are then unable to locate a handy toilet. It should be stressed that curtailing fluid intake is not usually a good idea and can have undesirable consequences in older people.

Urgency occasionally progresses to the stage of urge incontinence, when there may be sudden flooding. Usually, it predisposes to incontinence, and other factors actually precipitate it.

Precipitating factors

In elderly people these include the following:

(1) weakness of pelvic muscles (in women exercise may help for example stop in mid-stream and hold on);

(2) senile atrophic vaginitis—a course of oestrogen may help;

(3) cystitis—frequency of micturition, burning discomfort, and general unwellness may point to this possibility;

(4) diuretics—these frequently turn urgency into urge incontinence;

(5) tranquillizers and hypnotics—these may prevent the SOS message desperately being transmitted by the bladder from waking you up in time;

(6) constipation, especially if severe.

Treatment

Some of the factors mentioned above can be easily treated, even if the underlying bladder instability cannot. The nurse may suggest trying to retrain the bladder by instructing the patient to keep a chart and to start by emptying the bladder at two-hourly intervals throughout the day, increasing the interval when successful. Occasionally, drugs can be helpful. If the incontinence is refractory but not especially severe, pads can sometimes be sufficient, but otherwise a sheath-type appliance for men, or a catheter for either sex, will be necessary.

Overflow incontinence

Less commonly, incontinence can be due to difficulty in voiding urine which is occasionally unrecognized by the patient. Most people are familiar with acute retention which quite commonly afflicts men with prostatic enlargement, especially if given a powerful diuretic or following the consumption of three or four pints of beer. The condition is an exceedingly uncomfortable and sometimes agonizing one but sitting in a warm bath may permit the urine to flow. Otherwise, catheterization is required and relief is ecstatic: prostatic surgery may then be advised, particularly if there have previously been suggestive symptoms such as difficulty in initiating micturition, a poor stream, and dribbling. During the interval at the theatre, it is always advisable to queue behind the young men and not the old ones!

Not infrequently, enlargement of the prostate leads to chronic retention with overflow, producing a painless but grossly distended bladder containing perhaps 1.5 or 2 litres of urine. This results in a constant dribbling form of incontinence, and also damage to the kidneys through back-pressure. Other causes of outflow obstruction include urethral stricture and severe constipation. The same situation can arise if there is neurological disease affecting the micturition reflex, which may occur, for example, as a complication of diabetes or as a result of certain drugs which affect the nervous system. Treatment will be dictated by the cause, but if unsuccessful will again need to be by catheterization—occasionally intermittent, but more often on a long-term basis.

Aids and appliances

In the UK and many other countries it is now usual for there to be a continence advisory nurse practitioner who can advise concerning the different types of pads and pants available, so that comfort, ease of use, adequate absorption, and discretion are achieved. The object is to absorb the urine and yet keep the skin dry. She can advise men concerning the possibility of a sheath which drains into a bag attached to the leg, and will also be familiar with the absorbent bed sheets which are available. These sheets have to be purchased by the user but pads and pants are usually available through the community nurse. In the UK, the cost of incontinence can be mitigated through the attendance allowance or the invalid care allowance.

A catheter is acceptable to some patients but bitterly resented by others. It will probably only need changing every six weeks to three months. The catheter remains connected to a drainage bag which should be emptied at least three-hourly and changed every five to seven days. The patient is usually given two or three leg-fitting bags and two or three larger bedside drainage bags which can be attached to a thick wire stand. The flow should be downhill at all times and the area around the catheter needs daily washing; bathing or preferably taking a shower is perfectly possible.

16   Heart, blood vessels and lungs

Does the heart deteriorate?

As we have emphasized throughout this book, we still cannot distinguish between the intrinsic and inescapable effects of the passing years on the human body, the ravages of common age-related diseases, and the results of giving up physical activity on retirement or earlier. Viewed under the microscope, heart muscle does not alter much except for the accumulation of the brownish waste product called lipofuscin in the cells and deposits of another waste product, amyloid, between the cells. In general, these materials seem to be virtually harmless. The specialized network of cells which conducts the impulse to the different parts of the heart muscle to produce a co-ordinated heartbeat may be infiltrated by fibrous tissue, and this can have serious consequences as we shall see. Finally, the mitral and aortic valves may have deposits of calcium on their leaflets which can interfere with the effectiveness of the valves.

Nevertheless, the healthy heart continues to pump the blood around the circulatory system perfectly satisfactorily into extreme old age. It is widely accepted that the amount of blood pumped per minute declines because the output per beat is diminished, but it has recently been claimed that the cardiac output and the volume per beat do not inevitably fall in fit subjects spared coronary artery disease. Faced with the increased demands imposed by physical exertion, the old heart cannot respond with such a large increase in rate as a young one, and the maximum consumption of oxygen does seem to decline inevitably by 1 per cent a year from the age of 30 onwards. It may be true that the average woman of 75 is performing to her maximum aerobic capacity when simply walking at 3 mph (about 5 km per hour), but a fit person at 70 has the same oxygen carrying capacity as an unfit person of 30.

What is atherosclerosis?

The terms arteriosclerosis, atherosclerosis, and atheroma have very similar meanings and have traditionally been interpreted as 'hardening of the arteries', although narrowing of the arteries is at least as important a consequence. Atherosclerosis is the scourge of our time and is the leading cause of death in the developed nations, whether in the guise of coronary artery disease or of strokes. It affects the vessels supplying various parts of the body and these parts in turn sustain damage as a result of the reduction in their blood supply. There is patchy thickening of the arterial wall due to accumulation of platelets, cholesterol, and fibrous tissue, leading to a series of partial obstructions to the flow of blood. Sometimes the interior of the artery becomes totally blocked by atheroma, or by clotting of the blood due to the sluggishness of the flow, or by a microscopic leak of blood into an atheromatous plaque, or by a clump of platelets forming on an ulcerated patch and then detaching itself and lodging in a narrower branch downstream. The effects therefore vary according to the arteries involved and the degree of narrowing or occlusion. There may be an intermittently inadequate blood supply, for example when the demand for oxygen and nutrients is particularly high, or there may be total starvation. An organ or extremity denied sufficient blood is said to be ischaemic, and an area of tissue whose blood supply is cut off will die or undergo 'infarction'. As a rule, atherosclerosis is a generalized disease, but its clinical effects in the individual patient may be confined to one particular arterial territory.

Is atherosclerosis an inevitable concomitant of ageing?

Atherosclerosis is certainly related to ageing, but other factors influence its rate of progress. In certain societies, notably Japan, advanced coronary artery disease is uncommon in post-mortem studies of people well into their 60s. There are a number of well-known risk factors for developing arterial disease, some of which are capable of modification while others are not (see Table 16.1). Attention to those factors which we can influence has led to a fairly spectacular decline in mortality from the ravages of atherosclerosis in a number of countries, with the USA leading the way (see Figs 16.1 and 16.2).

What are the effects of atherosclerosis?

The main targets for this process are the brain, the heart, and the legs. Disease of the carotid and cerebral arteries produces strokes.

Sometimes minor, transient episodes known as transient ischaemic attacks (TIA) give a warning that a major stroke is threatened, and it may be possible for the physician to take action to try to avert such a disaster. If the coronary arteries are affected, the outcome may be a heart attack (coronary thrombosis, myocardial infarct) or it may be heart failure. If the vessels are narrowed but not occluded, the characteristic chest pain on exertion known as angina alerts us to the disease process, and there are various medical and surgical interventions which can influence the course of events. Similarly, arterial disease of the legs can cause pain in the calf on exercise when the oxygen requirements of the muscles are at their greatest (claudication) and it occasionally progresses, if unchecked, to gangrene.

Rather less commonly, the arteries supplying the kidneys and the intestine are affected, to the extent that clinical manifestations

Table 16.1   Risk factors for atherosclerosis (National Heart, Lung, and Blood Institute 1981).

INTRINSIC
  Cannot be modified
    Age
    Sex
    Genetic and familial influences

INTRINSIC BUT SUBJECT TO ENVIRONMENTAL INFLUENCE
  May be modified with likely benefit
    Hypertension
    Obesity
    Hypercholesterolaemia

  May be modified but benefit uncertain
    Diabetes mellitus

  Possibility of modification unknown
    Type A behaviour

ENVIRONMENTAL
  Benefit of elimination established
    Cigarette smoking

  Benefit of elimination not established
    Physical inactivity

occur, for example pain arising from the gut or diarrhoea. Yet another effect of the disease is the progressive expansion of the aorta in the abdomen to form a sac or aneurysm, with the danger of a sudden catastrophic rupture.

What happens to the blood pressure as we grow older?

In the developed countries, the blood pressure tends to rise until the 70s and then levels off or even declines. However, this rise is not an integral aspect of human ageing since it appears not to occur in Fijians or Amazonian Amerindians. In western societies, the prevalence of hypertension (over 160/90) in the age group 75–9 has been found to be over 40 per cent.

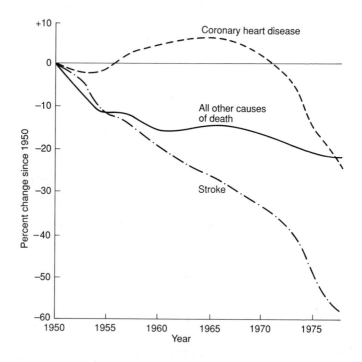

Fig. 16.1 Changes in mortality from coronary heart disease, stroke, and all other causes of death in the US, 1950–77.

Source: Levy, R. I. (1981). Declining mortality in coronary heart disease, *Arteriosclerosis*, **1**, 312–15.

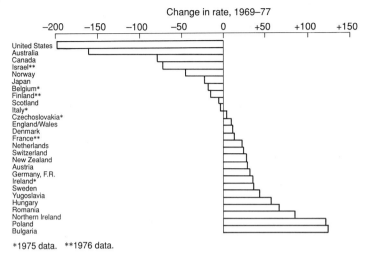

Change in rate, 1969–77

*1975 data.   **1976 data.

Source: Prepared by NHLBI; data from the World Health Organization.

Fig. 16.2 Changes in cardiovascular disease mortality, by country, 1969–77.

Source: Levy, R. I. (1981). Declining mortality in coronary heart disease, *Arteriosclerosis*, **1**, 312–15.

What is heart failure?

Heart failure can result from virtually every type of heart trouble, with coronary artery disease and high blood pressure being far and away the commonest causes in the western world. As the pumping action of the heart becomes feebler, it becomes unable to cope with all the blood being returned to it by the great veins (especially if there is increased resistance to forward flow), and a back pressure builds up. If this happens acutely, it affects primarily the lungs, which become waterlogged with fluid filling the air spaces (pulmonary oedema) resulting in rapidly progressive breathlessness. This medical emergency often comes on during the night. Although very frightening, it usually responds well to treatment.

Chronic heart failure is much less dramatic and is again the result of failure by the heart to cope with the blood returning to it so that there is back pressure throughout the circulation. The sufferer will notice that he is breathless on exertion and that the ankles are swelling due to accumulation of fluid. Treatment consists of diuretics to disperse the fluid and other drugs to lower resistance to flow through the blood vessels. Once again, the response is satisfactory although the underlying disease process has not been addressed.

Heart failure can also be precipitated by rhythm disturbances when the heart may beat too quickly or too slowly or irregularly, and these also may occur in any type of cardiac pathology.

Can heart disease be treated?

The treatment of heart failure has been mentioned, but tackling the underlying problem is obviously preferable. Effective drugs are available to treat high blood pressure (beta-blockers to counteract certain effects of adrenalin, calcium antagonists, Angiotensin Converting Enzyme (ACE) inhibitors). Angina can be treated medically, but the results of coronary artery bypass grafting are excellent and this procedure probably improves prospects for survival. Various abnormalities of the heartbeat may result from fibrosis of the conducting tissues, with the result that the beat is too fast, too slow, or irregular, and there are many drugs which can control these abnormal rhythms if they can be identified. This may be difficult because some of these disturbances are very transient, and merely result in 'coming over queer'. Under these circumstances, it may be necessary to record each heartbeat on a tape cassette attached to the body over a period of 24 hours. An excessively slow heartbeat is potentially dangerous and may result in very dramatic episodes of collapse with loss of consciousness for a minute or so: pacemakers for hearts that beat too slowly are highly effective. The replacement of defective valves is another worthwhile though much more major procedure. Successive myocardial infarcts can result in a failing pump with an inadequate output, and in 1988 one centre in the UK reported favourable results from heart transplantation among patients in their 60s.

Can diseased arteries be treated?

Aortic aneurysms can be excised and replaced by prosthetic grafts—preferably *before* they rupture. Blocked leg vessels, like coronary arteries, can often be surgically bypassed, or sometimes dilated using balloon catheters which are manipulated through the arterial system and inflated at the narrow segment. The most important measures, however, lie in correcting the risk factors and there is some evidence that atherosclerotic lesions can regress if the subject stops smoking, eats sensibly, and has his hypertension treated.

Do the lungs alter with age?

Considering that during our lifetimes we breathe in and out some 300 million litres of air, the lungs of even the remotest country dweller come into contact with a great deal of pollution, so that differentiating between environmental damage and true age change is almost meaningless. The area of the gas-exchange surface reaches about 80 square metres in our 20s and tends to shrink a little to perhaps 70 square metres at age 70. The lungs become stiffer, and so does the chest wall, causing us to use our diaphragms rather more than our thoracic muscles for breathing as we grow older. The rate and quantity of air we can blow out into a spirometer or a peak-flow meter also decline, and there is a slight reduction in the amount of oxygen carried in the blood.

Perhaps none of these physiological changes is particularly harmful, but one that probably is important is the decline in the defence system in the air passages. Particles of dust and bacteria become trapped in mucus in the bronchi and are swept back to the trachea by the beating action of the tiny hairs which project from the lining. Eventually, the mucus and the trapped matter is coughed up. This protective mechanism does seem to become less efficient in old people, rendering them more liable to lung infections.

How can bronchitis and pneumonia be avoided?

The most important step anyone can take to preserve the health of the lungs is to stop smoking and avoid the company of those who do smoke, and this remains highly advisable at any age. Other preventive measures can be taken. For example, when there is an epidemic of influenza, it is prudent to minimize the risk of contact with it by avoiding crowded public places. It is also recommended that people aged over 65 should seek vaccination against influenza in the early autumn each year. This is especially important for those at special risk on account of diabetes, chronic bronchitis, or asthma, or those living in communal establishments. There is also a vaccine available against the commonest form of pneumonia and these high-risk subjects would be well advised to ask their doctors about the benefits of receiving it, as perhaps should everyone over 65.

17   Eyes, ears, teeth, skin, and feet

There are very few life-threatening conditions which affect these areas. Nevertheless, there is no doubt about their importance. Any impairment of their function exposes a person to dangers and strips life of much of its pleasure.

People aged 75 or over in the United Kingdom now have the opportunity of an annual check of their health through their general practitioner. The areas covered by this chapter are probably those where most benefit can be gained in these checks.

Eyes

Blindness

Blindness may start as intermittent or permanent loss of vision. The permanent forms may come on suddenly or gradually. It is the transient episodes and gradual deterioration which are of greatest importance, as they have a greater chance of successful intervention and prevention of serious permanent impairment.

Intermittent blindness

Most fleeting episodes of blindness are due to abnormalities in the blood supply to the retina (light-sensitive part of the eye) or to the part of the brain which receives and interprets messages (the occipital region at the back of the brain) or the connecting nerve pathways. A reduction in blood flow may result from an alteration in the effectiveness of the circulation; a fall in blood pressure, or an alteration in the rate or rhythm of the heart may be responsible. The partial obstruction of a blood vessel may occur due to the passage of a small clot (embolus); this may arise from a damaged heart valve or roughened area on the wall of the heart or an artery. Thickened blood vessels in the eye are also more vulnerable as the consequently narrowed lumen is more easily blocked. This can happen in patients with arteritis, an inflammatory thickening of the artery wall. However, some of these conditions can be treated if detected. The brief loss of vision is therefore an important warning sign which, if ignored, may allow the underlying changes to progress to permanent blindness. It is therefore essential that such symptoms are reported to your doctor so that attempts can be made to identify precipitating factors, which hopefully can then be reversed before serious damage occurs.

Progressive blindness

Several of the slowly progressive causes of blindness can be corrected or checked. The difficulty in their management is lack of awareness of the problem. It is amazing how restricted a person's vision can become before the problem is appreciated; this is particularly true where it is the scope of vision (visual field) which has gradually shrunk.

Glaucoma

Chronic glaucoma is the best example. In this condition the pressure in the eye gradually increases and results in damage to the optic nerve. As the process progresses, the angle of vision becomes increasingly narrow, until the victim is effectively looking down a narrow tunnel (Fig. 17.1). Because details in that tunnel are clearly and precisely seen the patient can manage to lead a surprisingly normal life, until a critical point of visual loss has been passed when it is too late to regain the lost vision. Early signs of the problem are really non-existent although 10 per cent of victims will have a

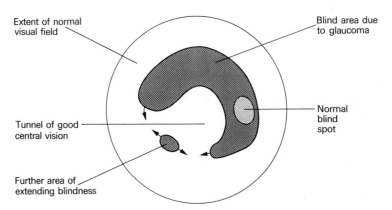

Fig. 17.1 Visual field of the right eye in a patient with glaucoma, progressing to complete tunnel vision.

family history of glaucoma. The only method of protection is regular eye testing, including the measurement of eyeball pressures. Eye tests for people with a relative with glaucoma are free of charge in the UK. Treatment in early cases consists of reducing the eye pressure by instilling drops which either help the drainage of the fluid from the eye (pilocarpine) or reduce the production of fluid (Diamox or timolol). In the latter stages, relief can only be obtained by a surgical operation to enable free flow and drainage of fluid inside the eye; a small cut in the iris is the usual technique.

There is also an acute form of glaucoma, and this is a dramatic medical emergency. The patient becomes acutely ill with headache, vomiting, and blurring of vision. The eye will appear red and angry, if the pressure is not relieved urgently in these eyes, then rapid blindness will result.

Cataract

A very common eye change in old age is cataract. This is a clouding of the lens which prevents light reaching the sensitive retina in the normal way. The condition accounts for about one-eighth of all ophthalmic out-patient appointments and half the department's operations. Although the condition is rare before old age, it can occur early in especially vulnerable groups like diabetics. Most patients are over 70 years of age. Once formed, the opacity persists and progresses and may eventually require removal. Much skill is required in deciding when the opaque lens is ripe and should be extracted. Postoperatively there are likely to be problems with adjustment to the new situation. Replacement lenses in the form of glasses cause considerable distortion of vision; this must be compensated for by the patient and is especially difficult if good vision remains in the unoperated eye. Contact lenses and lenses inserted into the eye give better vision and have fewer acceptance and tolerance problems as far as the patient is concerned. When to operate is clearly a matter for careful discussion between surgeon and patient, as is the question of local or general anaesthesia. Age alone is never a contraindication to surgery and the duration of hospital stay is usually very short or it can be done as a day case.

Destruction of the retina

Destruction of the light-sensitive retina is the third progressive form of blindness. To some extent atrophic ageing changes occur in this tissue in all elderly people. The back of the eye in old age—when seen through an ophthalmoscope—is paler than in youth. It tends to have a less abundant blood supply and extra amounts of pigment are to be seen scattered around the retina. Patients with long-standing or poorly controlled diabetes or high blood pressure are at extra risk. Bleeding into the back of the eye and the development of new blood vessels are further complications which can seriously damage vision. Diabetes is now the most common cause of blindness in the UK—either resulting from cataract formation or the destruction of the retina, or both together. The new blood vessel formation in diabetic eyes can be modified by laser treatment, and the same technique can be used in patients where the retina has become torn and detached; the laser burns are used in a controlled way to cause scarring and to prevent further damage.

Eye tests

It is normal for visual acuity to deteriorate with increasing age. It is therefore essential that the elderly arrange to have their eyes tested at regular intervals, thus ensuring that they always have the most suitable lenses in their glasses. Patients with diabetes, high blood pressure, or a family history of glaucoma must especially ensure that they receive routine examinations of their eyes and vision. Simple measures such as good lighting and clean spectacles or magnifying glasses should always be available and should not be dismissed as trivial.

Ears

Everybody knows that our ears are for hearing—but in addition they have the function of maintaining equilibrium. Ability to hear acutely tends to decline with age (a process known as presbycusis) and begins at the age of 30 years due to auditory nerve impairment. The perception of high-pitched sounds is most affected (Fig. 17.2). Differentiation between sounds is also impaired—this is an important loss in noisy surroundings—and in such circumstances it may be difficult to follow one conversation among many others. Perhaps this is one reason why overcrowded cocktail parties are more favoured by 'bright young things' than by mature sages!

The wax in our outer ears also changes with age, becoming

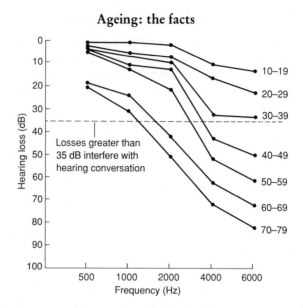

Fig. 17.2 Average audiograms for each decade of age.

harder and less likely to clear itself spontaneously. As it accumulates it may form a very hard plug which will effectively impair the transmission of sound waves down to the ear drum and onwards. When these two ageing phenomena occur together there can be very significant hearing loss.

It is therefore not surprising that deafness is common in old age. We do not really know how many people are affected but it has been estimated to be over one-third of those over 65, rising to half over 80 years of age. Unfortunately many accept it as a normal part of old age, and therefore do not seek help and remain handicapped, usually unnecessarily. About 125 000 people over 65 years of age are recognized as having impaired hearing in the UK alone. This is certainly only the tip of the iceberg, but they are probably the most severely affected.

Advice should be sought as the majority can be helped. Wax is easily identified by a doctor and can be painlessly syringed away after an initial period of softening with drops. Presbycusis can be overcome by the fitting of a hearing aid but this must be properly maintained.

Operations to free the internal mechanisms of the ear can also be performed when indicated. Patients needing such help often have a family history of deafness and will have themselves been afflicted probably in early middle age. Otosclerosis is the most common diagnosis in these circumstances, where articulating bones in the inside of the ear have become fused and need to be released so that they can more effectively transmit sound waves. These internal mechanisms can also become temporarily damaged during ear and throat infections; if permanent, surgical intervention will be required. Hearing aids are often very effective in minimizing any residual defects.

Some drugs—especially gentamycin and frusemide—are liable to damage hearing if given in excessive doses. The elderly are particularly vulnerable in this respect and care is needed in the use of these drugs in old age.

Helping people with deafness

The first stage is trying to understand their problems. Because they cannot hear properly does not mean that they live in silence. Usually they are constantly distracted by additional or distorted sounds. They feel very isolated, sometimes to the extent of being precipitated into mental illness. Both depression and paranoia are frequent problems in the deaf because the uncertainty about what is being said fosters suspicion.

Communication is made easier if the person talking speaks clearly and slowly. He should position himself so that the available light shines on his face, not from behind him. He should not obscure his mouth with a hand or other object, or turn away when talking. All extraneous noises and distractions should be abolished wherever possible.

A deaf person should not hesitate to inform a new acquaintance of his difficulty and to give advice about overcoming the problem.

Hearing aids

When there is concern about failing hearing, medical advice should be taken. Once simple difficulties like wax have been excluded, the patient's suitability for a hearing aid will be considered. However, it should not be expected that an appliance will restore hearing to normal. The aid must be fitted properly into the ear, it must be kept clean with intact and patent tubing and the batteries must always be 'live'. The volume of received speech will be amplified but distortions and extra noises will remain a problem. Special facilities can be provided to supplement a hearing aid; many public places, such as theatres, have installed a loop system which improves reception to an aid. In the UK British Telecom can fit an inductive coupler to telephones, an apparatus which helps to eliminate background noise when a hearing aid is used. It is UK policy for this adaptation to be installed in all public call boxes, and those currently altered can be identified by the World Deaf symbol. To benefit from this system it is necessary to have one of the new post-aural hearing aids which incorporate a three position switch. Telephone companies can also offer other forms of help to telephone users, such as additional ear-pieces so that both ears may be used, loudspeakers, volume controls for the telephone bell (or its replacement by a flashing light). The local telephone sales office can supply further information.

Tinnitus

This is a symptom which consists of noises in the ears. It may be continuous or intermittent and is usually associated with hearing impairment. In most cases the tinnitus is due to degenerative changes in the middle or inner ear but some cases are secondary to severe noise damage.

Tinnitus is an annoying symptom—it affects about 17 per cent of the UK population (but this incidence rises to 20 per cent in the over-65s). About 5 per cent of sufferers have severe symptoms and in 0.5 per cent they are incapacitating.

Treatment is difficult and often unsatisfactory. The provision of a hearing aid will sometimes help if the tinnitus is associated with deafness. Other patients may be helped by a masker—which produces 'white noise' which may override the tinnitus. Anxiety and tiredness often make symptoms worse, so stressful situations should be avoided if possible.

Teeth

In old age the main problem is lack of teeth. This is most unfortunate as careful maintenance and preventive measures should enable people to retain their own teeth to the end of life. It is interesting that in wild animals it is loss of teeth that leads to death through malnutrition and starvation. Fortunately, such a drastic outcome is avoided in humans. Most teeth are lost as a result of a complication of periodontal (gum) disease; chronic infection and retraction of the gums will leave the teeth loose and insecure. It is an advantage if even only a few teeth survive, so full-scale clearance should be avoided wherever possible. Any remaining teeth act as useful anchors for dental appliances, so a more snug and secure fit is likely to be obtained. In developed countries there is good evidence that the greater attention to dental care in recent years is showing significant benefit (Table 17.1).

Table 17.1 Results of Swedish dental survey.

1971–72 — 50% of 70-year-olds lacking own teeth
1976–77 — 40% " " " " " "
1981–82 — 30% " " " " " "

Dentures

Dentures may themselves cause many problems. Irritation due to roughness or poor fitting can lead to severe, persistent ulceration of the lining of the mouth. Poor occlusion of dentures can cause excess stresses and strains in the jaw and lead to painful arthritis of the jaw (temperomandibular) joint. Poor fitting can lead to collapse of the mouth with poor sealing of the lips, so that saliva may escape at the corners, and lead to areas of maceration and fungal infection at that site. It should be remembered that the mouth continues to change shape after dental extraction; in particular the bone ridges recede, and dentures may therefore become loose and need regular replacement. Lack of natural teeth does not mean that one no longer needs to attend the dentist! If there are difficulties in visiting the dentist, it may be possible to receive a domiciliary service or a mobile unit may be available. If such facilities are needed, contact should be made with the district health authority's dental officer (in the UK). Charges for dental treatment may present considerable difficulties to many elderly people. Treatment is only free to the elderly if they are receiving income support—however, six-monthly checkups, repairs to dentures, and emergency treatment are all free.

Skin

The skin in older people has a slower cell turnover than in youth. The cells are smaller in size and number; the results of these changes are thinner and drier skin, and the supporting tissues in the skin are also reduced in amount. Increased laxity in skin shows itself as wrinkles. The horizontal furrows across the forehead are the first to appear, some time after the age of 20 years. Next are crow's feet at around 40 years, then wrinkles around the corner of the mouth from 50 years, and ten years later creases around the lips start to appear. This timing has considerable individual variation as exposure to sunlight and weather generally tends to accelerate these changes.

Another consequence of the reduction of supporting tissue in the skin is the appearance of spontaneous areas of bleeding below the surface. These too are most likely to appear on exposed surfaces, especially the back of forearms and hands. They are quite harmless, insignificant, and painless.

Ageing skin also becomes drier and more scaly. These changes alone may be sufficient to account for the common complaint of generalized itching. Other causes, such as kidney failure, liver failure, severe iron deficiency anaemia, and endocrine disorders are much less common, and not specific to old age.

Spots, warts, and moles

Spots, warts, and moles all tend to increase in frequency in old age. Small cherry-red spots on the trunk—Campbell de Morgan spots—are common and harmless. Seborrhoeic warts (brown, unsightly plaques) may become widespread, but these rather horny nodules are of no significance. Moles may be sinister, especially if they bleed or rapidly increase in size, and help should be sought immediately. Similarly, it is important not to ignore persistent ulcerated areas on the face. Both of these conditions may be malignant but can often be easily cured. Skin cancers become more common with increasing age, especially on the head and neck, due to prolonged exposure to sunshine.

Diseases of the skin

Few skin diseases are specific to the elderly. Psoriasis can affect any age group and the majority of sufferers take their disease into their old age. Eczema can also affect any age group. Herpes zoster (shingles) can be very troublesome in old age. It is caused by the chicken-pox virus, and has usually been present since childhood but remained dormant. When resistance is low it may be roused and cause a very painful rash affecting either a segment of the body or one of the eyes and its surrounding skin. Antiviral preparations are now available to shorten the course of the illness and its severity. The relief of pain and protection of sight (if the eye is affected) are the main function of the supervising doctor.

Drug reactions affecting the skin, such as rashes and itching, are common in the elderly, mainly because they are the greatest users of medications.

Skin care

Skin care in old age should concentrate on cleanliness, but without excessive washing. Exposure to trauma should be avoided wherever possible as healing may be slow. Prolonged and fierce sunshine should be considered as traumatic.

Intertrigo

A particularly troublesome problem—especially in the obese and in hot conditions—is intertrigo. This consists of red, moist, sore, and smelly areas in skin folds, for example, under the breasts or in the groin. Although lack of hygiene is responsible, some cases are resistant to washing as the skin may be infected with fungal organisms, and applying antifungal preparations to the skin is the only way of clearing them. Vulval involvement can be the first sign of undiagnosed diabetes mellitus.

Leg ulcers

Leg ulcers become more frequent as people age, and are usually just above the ankle. In younger people they are nearly always a consequence of poor venous blood flow. The resulting stasis leads to breakdown of the skin surface. Normally they are painless, unless the surrounding skin becomes infected. In older people there is likely to be an element of poor arterial circulation due to narrowing of the arteries which supply that particular region; the subsequent oxygen lack may be the reason why these ulcers are more frequently painful in older victims.

The main principles of treatment are regular cleaning of the ulcer, bandaging to prevent local swelling, and intermittent elevation of the legs. Although prolonged periods of rest can be beneficial in the young, such an approach may be counterproductive in the elderly. In some cases plastic surgery is the best solution to ensure rapid and complete healing. Unfortunately these ulcers may still persist as a chronic and unsightly burden, in spite of attempts at healing.

Hair

Hair becomes finer, greyer, and less luxuriant as the years pass. The familiar male balding with receding hairline may also affect women, but only to a significant degree if they live into their 80s and 90s. A general thinning of head hair is the most common hair change in elderly women. Body hair also diminishes and greys, and tends to be lost in the opposite order to which it was gained—trunk first, then legs, and finally pubic and axillary hair. It is very rare for anybody to live long enough to become totally hairless! Conversely, increased hairiness is likely to affect the facial appearance of elderly women to the extent that 40 per cent of those over the age of 80 are likely to be troubled by excessive facial hair. This may reach such proportions that regular shaving becomes necessary.

Feet

Footcare is frequently neglected by both individuals and the health service. However, in old age discomfort from foot problems is very common (Table 17.2).

Table 17.2 Foot problems in people over the age of 80 living in their own homes.

Difficulty in cutting toenails	77%
Corns and calluses	58%
Nail problems	56%
Toenail deformities	48%
Painful feet	30%
Restricted walking due to foot problems	10%

Help is likely to be needed with foot care because nails become thicker and harder and therefore more difficult to trim. In addition, there may be difficulties in reaching your feet, seeing your feet and using potentially dangerous instruments. For many people the assistance of a friend will be sufficient. However, in those with particularly vulnerable feet, for example diabetics and patients with poor circulation in the feet, skilled help will be needed. Unfortunately chiropodists are in short supply and many of those who advertise themselves as such are not properly trained. If you are in one of the above risk groups, ensure that you attend only a registered chiropodist or a foot care assistant working under proper supervision.

18 Cancer

What is cancer?

Cancer and malignant disease are common names for a group of diseases characterized by excessive multiplication of cells of an abnormal type, resulting in one or more 'growths' (swellings or tumours) somewhere in the body. These cancerous diseases (malignancies) predominantly afflict the elderly but a few are more common in the young. With some cancers there is a strong inherited predisposition. The very high incidence of cancer in late life is thought to be due to a combination of a number of factors, especially:

(1) longer exposure to environmental hazards;

(2) reduced immune response to abnormal (malignant) cells;

(3) hormonal changes.

Not all new growths are cancers. *Benign tumours* consist of an excessive accumulation of cells, but the growth remains confined to the tissue of origin. *Malignant tumours (cancers)* comprise cell growths which are capable of invading the surrounding tissues and by entering the bloodstream and lymph channels can spread widely.

Diagnosis

Identification of the cancer, its extent, and the likely response to treatment can usually be gauged by ordinary medical examination, including blood tests and X-rays, supplemented when necessary by special scans to make images of selected parts of the body. Before treatment decisions are taken it is valuable to scrutinize suspect cells under the microscope using special staining techniques. The cells can be sucked out of the growth through a fine needle in many cases. For superficial disease, a smear or scrape from the suspicious area may suffice, as with the cervix. Sometimes cancer cells are found in sputum or urine. Specimens may also be secured through an endoscope, a device for looking into cavities of the body, such as the gut, bladder, and respiratory tract. Less often nowadays is it necessary to resort to surgical operation to secure tissue for examination. With the exception of cancer of the blood, it is not possible to make the diagnosis on a blood test, as is possible with some diseases. The identification of 'tumour markers' in blood is the subject of active research.

Manifestations of cancer (malignant disease)

The initial signal that all is not well can vary enormously, and can include the following:

1. A lump appears; the lump is found to be cancer.

2. Symptoms occur caused by the cancer, such as weakness, breathlessness, loss of appetite, loss of weight, bleeding, or pain; a lump may or may not be found by the doctor.

3. The function of some part of the body is disturbed due to the presence of a growth, for example there may be difficulty in swallowing, stomach trouble, or persistent bowel upset.

4. The cancer is revealed by a routine health check or by medical investigation undertaken on account of some other medical problem, such as an X-ray of the chest for pneumonia.

Despite popular belief pain is not a common presenting feature. It may occur later because of pressure on nerves, distension of internal organs, or weakening of bone structure. A bone may give way with no undue stress because it is eroded by cancer. Generalized wasting of the body is unusual early on in the disease but always occurs in the later stages. Anaemia is common and some cancers can bleed profusely, for example cancers of the lung and stomach. Patients with breast cancer, brain tumour, or leukaemia (a cancer of blood cells) tend not to waste until the disease is well advanced.

Generally, the behaviour of common cancers appears to be neither more nor less aggressive in older compared with younger people. The disease is the same, although the reaction of the host may be different. However malignant melanoma (a skin cancer) and thyroid gland cancer both appear to be more aggressive in the old, whereas cancer of the breast is usually less aggressive. The older person is more likely to have more than one malignancy or to have other diseases affecting heart, lungs, or kidneys. This extra burden of illness influences the outcome adversely and may limit treatment options.

How common is cancer in the elderly?

Over one half of all cases of cancer in the western world occurs in the population over the age of 65. Cancer accounts for a quarter of all deaths (Table 18.1) and the incidence and mortality increase rapidly with age (Fig. 18.1). Only diseases of the heart and blood vessels claim more victims (see Chapter 16). The ten most common sites for cancer are shown in Table 18.2. About one-third of all

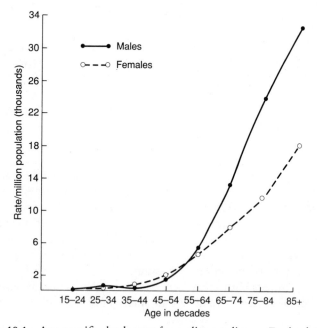

Fig. 18.1 Age-specific death rates for malignant disease, England 1985. *Source*: OPCS.

Table 18.1 Common causes of death
(Cambridge health district 1988).

Approximate % of total deaths	Males	Females
Heart disease	30	23
Cancer	25	26
Stroke	8	15
Chest disease	10	10

These figures, taken from the annual report of the Director of Public Health, Cambridge Health District, are similar to the UK average.

people will be affected eventually with some form of malignancy, males more than females and the elderly very much more than any other age group (Fig. 18.2).

Overall cancer incidence rates in the UK have been increasing for the last 50 years or so. Cancer of the lung in men has more than doubled, but is now falling; whereas in women the incidence has increased threefold and is still increasing—in some localities it may outstrip cancer of the breast. Lesser increases have been seen in postmenopausal breast cancer and in cancer of the pancreas, colon, bladder in both sexes, and prostate in men; all more prevalent in the old than the young. However there has been a reduction in

Table 18.2 The ten most common cancer sites (England and Wales 1984) as a percentage of all cancers

Men	%	Women	%
Lungs	26	Breast	22
Skin*	11	Skin*	11
Prostate	9	Lungs	10
Bladder	7	Colon	8
Stomach	7	Ovary	5
Colon	6	Stomach	5
Rectum, anus	5	Rectum, anus	4
Pancreas	3	Uterine cervix	4
Gullet	2	Uterine body	3
Kidney	2	Pancreas	3

* Excludes malignant melanoma
Source: OPCS 1984

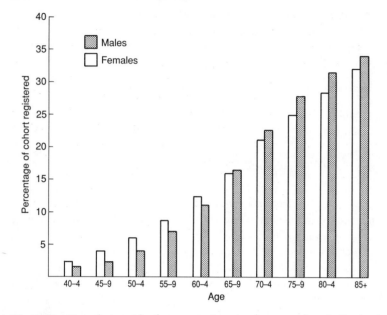

Fig. 18.2 Cumulative risk of cancer registration by age and sex in England and Wales, 1984.
Source: OPCS.

cancer of the gullet, stomach, rectum, and womb. The chances of dying from cancer are much greater for men than for women, for example the standardized age-adjusted mortality rate in England and Wales is about 284 and 179 per 100 000 population for males and females respectively. In the middle years women have the greater risk, but over the age of 60 years men are at greater risk, reflecting the higher fatality of male cancer as well as the higher incidence of the disease (Fig. 18.1).

Some possible causes of cancer

The precise cause is not known in most instances but a careful study of the prevalence of cancers in different groups within a community may reveal vital clues. Thus Percival Pott noted a marked increase in the incidence of scrotal cancer among chimney sweeps in the late eighteenth century. To avoid the cancer it was necessary to avoid the soot. Prevention could be effected even though the causative agent (carcinogen), a benzpyrene, was not identified until many years later. This work is a paradigm for studies in cancer causation and it shows the strong influence of the environment. A more recent example is the observation that cigarette smoking is associated with a marked increase in risk of developing cancer of the lung as well as a variety of other diseases.

Geographical variation also may give some clues. For example the incidence of breast cancer is high in the USA and low in the Orient. The incidence increases over two generations in those orientals who migrate to the USA. Contrariwise, cancer of the stomach is very common in Japan but relatively uncommon in the USA and the incidence in Japanese immigrants decreases over a generation or two. This suggests potent environmental influences in the host country. In general, cancer is more common in the north and west of the UK. Exceptions, where this north–south gradient is reversed, include cancers of the skin, prostate, and breast which are all more common in the south. Primary cancer of the liver is another disease which shows great geographical variation in incidence being very common in Africa and South-East Asia but rare in temperate climates. Chronic viral (hepatitis B) infection is the most important cause, especially in the Far East where chronic carriers of the virus have a risk of liver cancer—more than 200 times that of the uninfected population. The presence of cirrhosis of the liver due to alcoholism in men accounts for most of the cases in the UK. In some parts of Africa where liver cancer is common, not only is hepatitis B prevalent, but there are additional carcinogens in the diet, such as aflatoxin produced by fungi from badly stored grain and groundnuts.

It is estimated that 80–90 per cent of human cancer is related, at least in part, to exposure to environmental hazards. These may be chemical such as coal tar derivatives, physical such as radiation, or biological such as a virus. All these agents are capable of triggering the formation of cancer by their capacity to interact directly or indirectly with deoxyribonucleic acid (DNA) in the cell nucleus and so pervert cell organization. However, although all of us are exposed all of the time to multiple carcinogenic agents we do not all develop cancer. Other factors such as genetic inheritance predispose the individual to malignant disease. Some genes render a person more vulnerable. For example lung cancer is 30 per cent more likely to develop in the 10 per cent of individuals with a particular genetic make-up. Multiple polyps in the large bowel may occur as an inherited condition which runs in families. Although these tumours are benign when they first appear in youth, they usually become cancerous later and the victims die in middle age. Other genes appear to confer relative immunity to some forms of cancer and the absence of the protective gene or genes allows the carcinogen(s) to provoke the development of the malignancy. Retinoblastoma, affecting the eye in childhood, is considered to be caused in this way.

Cancer of the cervix (the neck of the womb) is thought to relate to sexual activity and there is information which suggests the human papillomavirus (HPV) is commonly, but not necessarily, implicated in the disease. Promiscuity, male as well as female, increases the chances of transmission of the carcinogenic agent(s). There is increasing evidence that viruses are implicated in the causation of a number of malignancies, including cancer of the liver as was explained above, either directly or as co-factors. Viral particles can sometimes be demonstrated inside the tumour cell. The cause of breast cancer is unknown. There are some recognized risk factors, but nothing so strong as the association of smoking with the development of lung cancer. Factors include: family history of breast disease, early onset of menstruation, higher than average maternal age at first full-term pregnancy, obesity, and late menopause. However absence of all these factors by no means eliminates the risk.

Delayed diagnosis in the elderly

Older folk (and their advisers) may ignore the warning signs and symptoms of cancer such as feeling off-colour, alteration of bowel habit, poor appetite, and weight loss. These symptoms may be attributed to 'growing old', feeling down in the dumps, or whatever. Lack of screening is another reason for delay in diagnosis.

Despite cancer being so common in late life, screening for cancer tends to stop much earlier. Cervical smears and routine pelvic and breast examinations are rarely performed in women over 65 despite the fact that cancer of the breast, uterus (cervix and body), and ovary all have their highest incidence and mortality in the over-70s. Vulval cancer is uniquely a cancer of extreme old age. Cancer of the prostate, the quintessential cancer of old age in men, can often be diagnosed by a simple rectal examination. Failure to screen means that these malignancies are commonly far advanced when the diagnosis is first made. This *laissez-faire* approach is inexcusable in otherwise well elderly people. In the UK, the recent introduction into the NHS contract for general practitioners of annual health checks for the over-75s is a step in the right direction.

Treatment prospects

Usually fit old people withstand medical investigations and treatment very well. For an otherwise fit old person, untreated cancer could cause a major shortening of life and, worse still, can severely degrade the quality of life remaining. Partial remission or complete remission of short duration may be quite sufficient to achieve a worthwhile prolongation of life of an acceptable quality. In late life the remission may well be long enough to allow death from some other cause.

Since curable cancers are in the minority, palliation is the mainstay of treatment at all ages; the primary goal being the relief of suffering. Unfortunately, many anti-cancer treatments are themselves distressing, especially major surgery, large doses of radiotherapy, or anti-cancer drugs. Prior discussion between doctor, patient, and family is necessary to allow full understanding of what is on offer and what might reasonably be expected from the intervention. Not surprisingly, some patients opt for symptom relief only.

In some circumstances surgical operation may be the best way to relieve symptoms, rather than rely solely on anodyne drugs. This could be so when colicky pain, vomiting, and blood loss are due to cancer of the colon. Although chronological age does not preclude surgery it does pose problems because of the loss of functional reserves especially in the heart and circulation, lungs, and kidneys as well as in the overall ability to make a reasonable recovery following any major procedure. Despite these uncertainties, major surgical intervention is often better tolerated than the more chronic stresses of extensive radiotherapy or intensive chemotherapy. Elderly tissues withstand radiotherapy less well than young and the aged bone marrow, vital for blood cell formation, is particularly sensitive to damage by radiation and drugs. Doses must be adjusted accordingly. Hormonal treatments are generally well tolerated and commonly employed for breast or prostate cancer.

What is the best cancer treatment for old people?

At any age the actual treatment depends primarily on the type and extent of the cancer but with allowance made for the likely response of the patient. Because most studies of cancer treatments have focused on the young and middle-aged, the best treatment for the very old is often not known. Much is left to inspired guesswork and 'playing safe'. There is a need to set up prospective studies to establish the best way to treat the common malignancies of the elderly. Patients with localized cancer usually are best treated with surgery if this is practicable, except for some common skin cancers which respond very satisfactorily to local applications.

Two or more different types of treatment may be used in combination, as well as with general measures to maintain the well-being of the patient. The doctor has to estimate how extensive the disease is to see if it is reasonable to aim for a 'cure', which in this context means a substantial remission, or to decide on a lesser aim if the treatment to produce the cure would be worse than the disease. For most patients, worthwhile palliation is the aim. Happily the myth of universal hopelessness traditionally attached to cancer is gradually giving way to more positive thoughts by doctors and patients alike.

Prospects for prevention and cure

It has been suggested that up to 90 per cent of cancers can be attributed to potentially avoidable factors, such as tobacco, alcohol, diet, sexual behaviour, occupational hazards such as radioactive substances, asbestos and aniline dyes, as well as to atmospheric pollution and exposure to sunlight. Thus changes in lifestyle and avoidance of environmental hazards are the main planks of prevention. When the level of proof is sufficiently high, appropriate advice can be given to people to reduce the risks. This is already possible with respect to some cancers affecting the skin, lungs, and urinary tract. Further research is needed to widen the scope of prevention. The omens look good in this regard.

In the meantime, since it is not yet clear how to avoid the majority of cancers, early detection and proper treatment are the best means of reducing the toll of illness and death. Screening programmes have been set up in a number of countries to attempt early detection of the more common cancers. Unfortunately, as pointed out above, the tendency is to direct the programme towards those under the age of 65. This ageist approach omits from the programme more than half the potential cancer victims.

Improved methods of detection and treatment become available year after year. Many currently used drug treatments will be replaced by more effective and much less toxic alternatives. More accurate delivery systems will be devised using both invasive and non-invasive techniques. For example, antibodies against tumour cells can be produced to act as carriers to deliver anti-cancer agents precisely to where they are needed and thus minimize damage to healthy tissue. These 'magic bullets' would be able to hit the target reliably and exclusively. We look forward to developments in cancer therapy with cautious optimism.

19   Medicines

In later life many of us suffer from one or more chronic disorders especially of the heart, lungs, nervous system, digestive tract, or of bones, muscles, and joints which may interfere with our daily lives. In the 1988 General Household Survey of England and Wales, of the sample aged 75 years and over, 68 per cent reported long-term illness, 53 per cent reported some limitation of activity on this account and 20 per cent had consulted their general practitioner (GP) in the previous 14 days. The presence of multiple disorders demands much medical attention and so the elderly are the chief consumers, the main beneficiaries, and when things go wrong, the main victims of modern pharmaceuticals. Since the media thrive on disaster, adverse effects of medicines are brought to public attention much more diligently than everyday beneficial effects. This may go some way to explain the paradox of a growing undercurrent of apprehension about modern medicine at a time when more and more people seek medical treatment and when benefit is more likely to ensue.

There is an apparently insatiable demand for medicines to treat the multitude of ills that old people are heir to. In the UK, the 18 per cent of the population who are of retirement age receive almost 40 per cent of the medicines dispensed in the National Health Service. The annual average number of NHS prescription items per elderly person has increased by more than 25 per cent since 1977. This age group is not charged for medicines prescribed under the state scheme in the UK. Modern medicines confer benefit in a wide range of common and serious diseases. A few are spectacularly successful, many give a reasonable degree of improvement, some are disappointing, and the odd one turns out to be disastrous.

It remains axiomatic that 'there is no pill for every ill' and much relief from suffering comes by other means. Drug treatment like so many other commodities such as food, water, gas, and electricity can never be entirely devoid of risk. Nevertheless when we are ill we are prepared to take some risk with medicines if they might make us feel and function better, and possibly be less dependent upon others. Most of us are prepared to take an even bigger risk if the disease is life-threatening. It is the work of pharmacologists to research and develop new medicines, it is the task of doctors to prescribe for maximum benefit with minimum risk, and it is for patients to realize that there are limitations to what medicines can be expected to accomplish.

Good medical treatment

The key to good medical treatment is accurate diagnosis of all components of the illness and an understanding of the likely response to drugs. The doctor can then select the medical priorities for treatment and discuss these with the patient, and if necessary with any supporting relatives or friends, indicating the anticipated benefits and the more common adverse effects. The ideal drug treatment should be highly efficacious and very safe but almost always some risk/benefit compromise has to be accepted. Most illnesses are readily dealt with by the general practitioner, but if diagnosis and management are not straightforward then specialist investigation is required.

Age alone is virtually never a bar to medical (or surgical) treatment and very few of us actually want to die when beleaguered by illness, whatever our age. What we do want is relief from distress and if possible improved function, but certainly not simply a prolongation of the business of dying. Happily the pharmaceutical companies have by processes of serendipity, trial and error and, more recently by design, produced many preparations which do relieve distress and on occasion transform the lives of elderly people. Parallel with these developments it has become increasingly recognized that treatment in elderly patients tends to be complicated by the combined effects of multiple drug use and altered patient responses due to ageing and disease.

The development of new medicines

Very many of the medicines prescribed today did not exist 30 years ago. Much meticulous research over a period of years takes place before a new medicine is marketed. Among the newcomers, preparations of particular value to ill older people include several antibiotics and a whole range of treatments for heart disease,

arthritis, mental disorders, Parkinson's disease, and some gastrointestinal disorders including peptic ulcers and constipation.

Before marketing a new drug, the pharmaceutical company must
produce convincing evidence to the govermental regulatory agencies of efficacy and likely toxicity of the new product. Initial tests
in animals are followed by tests in healthy human volunteers and
nowadays these must include elderly subjects if the drug is later to
be used in elderly patients. But sick elderly people do not always
respond to drugs in the same way as do the subjects in the pre-
marketing trials and so the early clinical trials have to be very
carefully supervised to assess the hazards as well as the benefits.
Unfortunately even this cannot guarantee success on general release
of the new drug because the numbers of patients treated in a clinical
trial can never equate with the tens of thousands or millions who
will use the drug once an acceptable level of efficacy and safety has
been demonstrated. Thus a drug found to be reasonably safe and
effective in a clinical trial involving a few score of patients later
turns out to have unacceptable toxicity when it comes into general
use. Because of these difficulties doctors in the UK are encouraged
to report to the Committee on Safety of Medicines any adverse
effects which have occurred in relation to all newly introduced
drugs.

The most dangerous drugs are taken off the market, for example
five antirheumatic drugs were withdrawn from the UK market
between 1982 and 1984. Others are permitted for restricted use
under specialist guidance or are given general release to all prescri-
bers, and the least toxic may be cleared for over-the-counter sales,
without prescription. The degree of availability of both prescribed
and over-the-counter medicines varies from country to country.
Sometimes, despite toxicity, it is reasonable to continue to use a
prescription drug if no safer alternative is available, and if the risk/
benefit ratio is acceptable to the patient. Common examples of
hazardous but still valuable medicines include digoxin (used to
control the heart rate), steroids (to treat a variety of serious
immunological disorders), and anticoagulants (to reduce clotting of
the blood). At other times it might be possible to avoid the adverse
effects by the concomitant use of another preparation, as is done
routinely with the modern treatment for Parkinson's disease, which
combines levodopa with an enzyme inhibitor. The concurrent use
of anti-ulcer drugs with certain antirheumatic drugs (the non-

steroidal anti-inflammatory drugs or NSAIDs) is being explored in an attempt to reduce gastrointestinal damage. It has been found that 50 to 60 per cent of patients on long-term treatment with NSAIDs complain of indigestion and from 10 to 20 per cent develop stomach ulcers. Yet NSAIDs have proved so helpful in the relief of symptoms of arthritis that millions of prescriptions for this class of drug are issued annually and more than three-quarters of the recipients are elderly. However, increased knowledge of the risk of adverse effects has led to a fall in enthusiasm for these preparations in recent years.

Drug use by the elderly

Our use of prescribed medicines (drugs) is likely to increase as we grow older and suffer from one or more of the common chronic illnesses of later life. Fig. 19.1. Consequently, drugs for the heart and circulation and for pain relief, especially in arthritis, as well as psychotropic agents (hypnotics, sedatives, tranquillizers, and anti-depressants) are prescribed on an enormous scale and account for

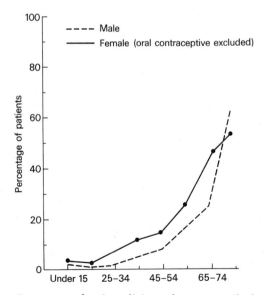

Figs. 19.1 Percentage of patients living at home prescribed medicines for 90 days or more. (After Murdoch 1980.)

about 50 per cent of all prescribing. In the main, their use is palliative rather than curative, as in the treatment of rheumatic complaints which afflict almost half the elderly population and account for about one-third of all general practice consultations in the over 65s. Of those aged 75 or more, 70–80 per cent are taking prescribed medicines and more than one-third of the women are on psychotropic medication, mostly on long-term repeat prescription. In addition many of us self-medicate using over-the-counter preparations, especially for pain, coughs, colds, and constipation.

Taking the medicine

More than 90 per cent of medicines come as tablets or capsules to be swallowed with food and drink, usually at mealtimes. A few medicines need to be taken with water only, separately from food, to allow adequate absorption from the bowel. The doctor or pharmacist will say when this special situation exists. It is not uncommon to encounter difficulty in swallowing pills. This can usually be overcome by swallowing the tablets along with food already softened in the mouth, while in an upright, sitting or standing, position and followed by at least half a cup of fluid taken over the next few minutes. 'Bedtime' drugs are best taken some 10–15 minutes before lying flat so as to avoid the tablets sticking in the gullet. Even when liquid medicines are taken, time should be allowed for them to reach the stomach before lying down. Less commonly, medicines are taken by other routes such as by inhalation for asthma, injections for diabetes, drops for eye troubles and by means of patches applied to the skin, by suppository, enema, or vaginal pessary.

Just what the doctor ordered

For most of us, taking the medicines, more or less as the doctor ordered, is no problem; but for those with marked mental or physical handicap the involvement of another person is required and there may need to be some compromise regarding times and modes of administration to suit both patient and helper. Fortunately, for most medicines the precise times are not critical although there are some important exceptions, as with levodopa in the later stages of Parkinson's disease and insulin injections in relation to meals in those with diabetes.

When we are ill we want to know what is wrong and what the

The tablets	Names and strengths	Purpose	To be taken
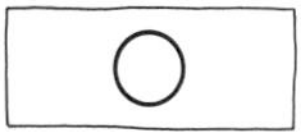 ○	Digoxin 125 mcg	heart	1 at breakfast
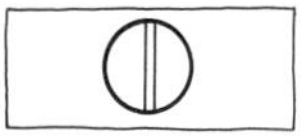 ⊕	Navidrex 500 mcg (cyclopenthiazide)	water	1 at breakfast
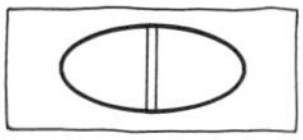 ⬭	Sinemet–Plus	Parkinson's	1 at breakfast
	Sinemet–Plus	Parkinson's	1 at lunch
	Sinemet–Plus	Parkinson's	1 at supper
 ⊘	Amitriptyline 25 mg	nerves	1 with drink 1/2 hour before bed

Fig. 19.2 Medication display chart.

Source: Coni, N., Davison, W., and Webster, S. (1988). *Lecture notes on geriatrics* (3rd edn). Blackwell, Oxford.

medicines are supposed to achieve. We also need clear instruction in the use of our medicines. If we need help with this task our helpers also must be instructed. When necessary, the pill-taking routine can be clarified by means of typed instructions or a medicine display chart where examples of each pill are fixed to a card with Sellotape alongside the essential information (Fig. 19.2). It is not uncommon to forget to take one's medicines and, on occasion, to forget that one actually has taken them! Taking the medicines at mealtimes and shortly before bedtime provides useful cues. Additionally, compartmentalized pill boxes are available which hold a day's, or a week's, supply of tablets and capsules, but they are not suitable for other types of medicines. For example, the Dosett has seven main compartments and each of these is subdivided into four, for different times of the day. Each day has its own sliding lid and the days and times are all clearly labelled, including labels in Braille. The contents are visible through the transparent

lids and instructions regarding the medicines are entered on to a
card which slides under the clear plastic of the base. Detailed
instructions for use are provided with the device. These boxes are
difficult for people with very stiff or clumsy hands. For those who
take their medicines while at home it may be convenient to have
each day's supply set out in open containers such as eggcups,
saucers, or even the base of an egg box. However, there is evident
risk with these homely arrangements if others, especially children,
have ready access to the pills.

A great potential for muddle exists when someone on multiple
drug treatments is discharged from hospital, because the supply of
medicines given to take home may be different from that in use
prior to admission. Vigilance by all concerned is required, more
especially since admission to hospital might actually have been due
wholly or in part to unsuitable drug therapy! Hoarding of drugs is
common because so many of us do not take pills as the doctor
ordered but rather as we think fit, and surplus medicines are kept
just in case they are needed. There are dangers in hoarding because
preparations can deteriorate with time, becoming either inactive or
even toxic. In addition, some drugs provide a temptation to young
drug abusers who may obtain supplies from the elderly by purchase
or theft. Unwanted medicines should be returned to the pharmacist
for destruction.

A short course of treatment such as an antibiotic for a chest
infection should be taken in full even though it is tempting to stop
as soon as one is feeling better. Long-term treatments require
review by the doctor and the frequency of the review will depend
upon the need. For instance a newly diagnosed diabetic prescribed
insulin or someone in severe heart failure would be seen frequently,
whereas those stable on long-term treatments, such as those for
pernicious anaemia or thyroid failure, may have just an annual
review. The general practitioner will have a computerized recall
system, or one based on a card index, to stop people 'falling
through the net'. However if you think you may have been
overlooked and you are on long-term repeat prescriptions, ask to
see the doctor.

If you have to take medicines

1. Obtain clear (preferably typed) instructions from your doctor
   or pharmacist.

2. Take your medicines regularly as instructed; report all unwanted effects.

3. Keep your medicines safe from: damp, heat, direct sunlight, and use by others, especially children.

4. Discard unwanted drugs; ask your doctor or pharmacist about this.

Response to medicines in elderly people

The response to medicines is essentially the same as in the younger adult. For example treatment of those diseases which usually respond well in younger patients (such as certain infections or thyroid failure) can be expected to give good results in old people also. Likewise diseases for which there is no cure but some palliation in the young (for instance chronic bronchitis or osteo-arthritis) can be expected to respond similarly in the elderly. The main differences in response of the aged person relate to:

(1) multiple drug use;

(2) altered body composition;

(3) reduced ability to eliminate toxic substances;

(4) altered sensitivity to some drugs;

(5) reduced reserve capacity due to ageing or disease.

Multiple drug use is prevalent in the elderly, partly because many common diseases each have multiple concurrent drug treatments and also because chronic diseases are often multiple in the one individual. Drug–drug interactions may occur, which can increase or decrease the desired effects of the preparations used. Mostly these interactions are of no significance, sometimes they are bene-ficial, but in certain circumstances they can be hazardous. In old people the kidneys and liver are smaller and less efficient in ridding the body of waste products, and the active tissues of the body, as opposed to the relatively inert body fat, are generally reduced. To allow for these factors doses are reduced. Frequently doses have to be scaled down still further to allow for the markedly impaired capacity for drug elimination from the body which occurs in liver and kidney disease and in states of dehydration.

Increased sensitivity appears to develop with ageing in the case of some drugs and smaller doses may be required on this account; as for example with benzodiazepines used as tranquillizers and hypnotics, and with warfarin used to prevent blood clotting. Reduction in the body's capacity to maintain a constant internal physical and chemical environment and reduction in functional reserves may mean that side-effects insufficient to cause upset in a young person can prove to be calamitous in an elderly one. Thus if there is already considerable reduction of brain and muscle function or in balance, an apparently innocuous prescription may precipitate mental confusion or a fall.

Modern medicines are a great boon to ill elderly people. Nevertheless, they do not resolve all life's problems and the utmost care is needed to secure maximum overall benefit.

20 Caring for an infirm elderly person at home

Through the ages the sick have looked to their families for succour and rarely have they been disappointed. Sooner or later, unless death comes suddenly, we will all need looking after on account of illness or disability. Before then, we ourselves are likely to be carers and for many the caring will last for months or years. This chapter has the needs of carers in mind, especially those who care for a heavily dependent relative. Around one-third of people over the age of 65 years living at home require help with one or more simple *domestic tasks* such as shopping, cooking, or routine housework. The proportion needing this help rises steeply with age. In the main the help is given by close relatives, including the spouse if there is one, although husbands characteristically display less zeal for domestic chores than do wives! Neighbours and friends may be helpful. In the UK the local authority may provide some community care services such as visits by a community care assistant (home help) and a meals on wheels service.

A similar proportion of the over 65s also requires help with movement around the house and with one or more *personal care tasks* such as washing, dressing, use of toilet, cutting toenails, and cutting up food and feeding. Over the age of 85, the vast majority of people require help with one or more of these personal care tasks. As for domestic work, help may come from the community care assistants for simple matters of hygiene and dressing but from the district nursing service for more specialized personal care procedures, for example with incontinence and pressure-sore management.

In a survey of 101 carers looking after 102 elderly dependent people (72 female and 30 male) living in and around Cambridge, it was found that common causes of dependence were arthritis and rheumatism, muscle weakness, liability to fall, heart trouble, strokes, forgetfulness, and more serious loss of mental faculties.

Table 20.1 Common disabilities of elderly dependents.

	Number affected
Arthritis and rheumatism	66
Incontinence of urine (faeces)	38 (22)
Total or partial blindness (deafness)	35 (44)
Mental depression	33
Dementia	27
Stroke	25
Disease of heart and circulation	31
Parkinson's disease	8

Survey of 72 female and 30 elderly dependants, all but four were age 66 or more.

Source: Bell, E., Gibbons, S., and Pinchen, I. (1987). *Action research with informal carers of elderly people: patterns and processes in carers' lives.* Addenbrooke's Hospital, Health Promotion Service, Cambridge.

About 40 per cent of the dependents were incontinent of urine and a smaller proportion were incontinent of faeces (Table 20.1).

It is in the nature of things that most dependent elderly people are female and an even higher proportion (about 80 per cent) of the carers are also female. Most of the carers are middle-aged (45–64 years), usually they are married, and some still have children at home. Many carers are themselves elderly and not always in the best of health. Almost always the key carer is the daughter or daughter-in-law and generally she lives in the same house or very near. Others have to make repeated car journeys to be with the dependent relative, or the decision might be taken to have the sick elderly person move into the carer's home. This eliminates the travelling and late night 'panic calls' but creates other stresses within the carer's family, if for example, all family life becomes subordinate to the needs of the dependant, the sitting room becomes the sick room, and bad smells pervade the house.

Prolonged caring can be enormously stressful both to the carer and to her family. On the other hand where the caring is the result of a deliberate choice by the carer the work can give great satisfaction, especially if unstinting support comes from family, neighbours, and the statutory authorities. A good sense of humour in all parties and a strong sense of personal worth in the carer are invaluable in maintaining morale.

Stress on the carer

Multiple stresses may occur as the months and years of caring roll by. These can be emotional, physical, financial, and social. The health of the carer may be adversely affected if the total burden of care is too great. She may have to abandon her usual social activities and perhaps feel obliged to give up a satisfying remunerative career. As the demands of caring increase, something has to give to accommodate the extra worry, physical work, long hours, and broken nights. The relentless demands of caring are such that some carers have not had a day off, let alone a holiday, for years, either because no alternative care was available (or not known to be available) or because the infirm person declined to have a surrogate carer in the house, refused to attend a day-care facility, and rejected a short spell in another household or an institution. The carer may have guilt feelings about requesting help, especially respite care, whether in the independent or public sector.

Financial pressures may build up because of the additional costs of heating, lighting and cooking, use of telephone, laundry, and transport. Even when the need exists, sick old people and their carers often do not utilize fully the available local care services and do not claim all the financial allowances to which they are entitled. The reasons are complex but include many factors such as a pride in coping and a desire to maintain privacy. It may also stem from apathy or ignorance, or simply a lack of assertiveness in approaching authoritarian health and welfare agencies. Also the intense loyalty of the carer may allow the demands of the dependant to take precedence over her own needs.

The carer is not infrequently tortured by the excessive and frequently conflicting demands put upon her. Fatigue, frustration, resentment, anger, anxiety, and guilt combine to tear at her emotions and make her life a misery. Devotion to her charge may lead her totally to ignore her own needs even though she knows, and will be reminded by family and friends, just what those needs are. She needs more time out, needs to distance herself a little, and requires others to share the burden of care. Family relationships become strained because the carer has no time or energy for them. 'You must decide between me and her' the exasperated husband declares, fuelling his wife's anguish.

Additionally there may be a change in the demeanour of the dependant as time and the progression of disease take their toll. Especially common is increasingly demanding behaviour, where the dependant cannot bear to be left alone and in peremptory fashion demands 'do this' or 'do that', always expecting immediate attention. Worse still, instead of expressing gratitude for the care given, the patient may say and do hurtful things. Not uncommonly the carer is compared unfavourably with a relative living at a distance who visits infrequently but is 'all sweetness and light' on those occasions. The old person may even have her will made out mostly to the benefit of the non-caring relative. In addition, the sight of a once strong, dominant personality becoming progressively weaker, weepy, incontinent, and generally incapable arouses feelings of distress and grief in the carer. The element of 'role reversal' can make for additional stress in the relationship because the daughter is now 'in charge' of the mother and may model her style of caring on her mother's earlier behaviour. It may be easier for a daughter-in-law or other helper to manage a 'difficult' elderly person.

Not surprisingly, a carer can reach a crisis point when she is liable to do harm to herself or to her charge. Abuse of elderly dependent people is common and takes many forms, ranging from scolding to serious physical assault. If the carer is anywhere near this stage it is imperative that she gives vent to her feelings in an innocuous way by leaving the room and expressing her anger in private, maybe by punching and screaming into a pillow, going for a walk, or whatever she finds releases tension. She must seek further help urgently, initially through her GP, the Samaritans, or a social worker to sort out the priorities fo care and to set limits to her caring. The distraught carer needs proper counselling and increased support. She should share her concerns with a close relative or trusted friend and have this person accompany her to the doctor or local office of the social services department when she petitions for help. Alternatively the local branch of Age Concern or the Citizen's Advice Bureau might be able to secure an advocate for her. These bodies also have extremely informative leaflets to guide carers.

Support for the carer

With good support, caring should not develop into the oppressive experience outlined above. In the main, support comes from the family and this may prove sufficient. The inadequately supported carer, however, needs to be able to sit down with a well-motivated, knowledgeable 'key worker' or 'care manager' from the health or social services and negotiate a suitable package of care. This package depends upon the needs of both carer and cared for; it also depends on availability of services, and these are of variable quantity and quality in different localities. The process of assessment and allocation of resources should be repeated at intervals as the circumstances change. This logical approach, which sadly is not yet the norm, is essential if chaos is to be avoided. Hopefully new legislation relating to community care in UK will promote the development of the domiciliary 'key worker' or 'care manager' role. Usually the family doctor calls in help from health or social services as appropriate, but is not involved in all the details of day to day management of the 'care package'. There is conflict if the sick old person takes precedence over the carer, who may herself be unwell but not on the same doctor's list. The carer must have her own advocate in these matters. A care manager could provide this essential service and help the carer to set limits to her caring. Failure to set limits almost always results in nature doing the job by rendering the carer too ill to continue and may lead to abuse of the dependant. Stress-related illness such as asthma, migraine, and high blood pressure are all quite common among long-term carers, as is back trouble, often due to unskilled lifting.

If you are a carer

If you are a carer you should find out from the doctor what is wrong with your patient, how things might progress, what treatment is being given, and what outcome is expected. You might ask the district nurse for some tuition in basic nursing skills, for example patient hygiene including the use of incontinence appliances, how best to feed your patient or move her from bed to chair or whatever is required. An occupational therapist from the local authority social services department could advise you on suitable aids to daily living and arrange for their provision and some tuition in their use. Items to be considered might include adaptations to clothing, bathing aids (such as firmly fixed hand-rails, bath-board and seat), eating utensils such as special cutlery for feeble arthritic hands, a commode and adaptations to the WC to facilitate toileting, and maybe a special mattress or particular type of bed, possibly with an overhead hand grip. Mobility may be improved by provision of a walking frame and training in its use by a physiotherapist. So many things have to be orchestrated that the care manager is vital to the success of the whole enterprise. In the more difficult cases she may well suggest involvement of the local hospital geriatric service or psychogeriatric service as appropriate.

Find out about extra help

You should also ask about the availability of alternative sources of care such as a community care assistant (home help), meals on wheels, and home nursing (Table 20.2). To allow you time out a

Table 20.2   UK Community care services

Health services	Social services
Family doctor	Community care organizer
Health visitor	domestic help
District nurse	personal care
Community psychiatric nurse	meals on wheels
Physiotherapist	sitting in service
Chiropodist	Social worker
Hospital geriatric and psychogeriatric day care and in-patient care	Day centre
	Residential home

There is also a wide range of voluntary and private care agencies.

'sitter' service and day care attendance for your charge are valuable. From time to time, respite care with a relative or friend or a spell in a local institution or possibly foster care with another family should be considered. It is wise to have a broad network of care so as to avoid being hopelessly trapped in the process of caring. Time out may be most needed when it is most difficult to achieve! We all know of amiable, gregarious, optimistic old people who attract lots of friends and relations to help with the caring. Such a person may gladly attend a day hospital or accept a stay with another family or in some form of institution just to give her principal carer a break. But how do you cope with the egocentric, morose, or cantankerous patient whose behaviour drives away the very support she needs and who refuses respite care? She may be adamant that she 'will not have strangers in the house', will not be 'bumped around to attend day hospital', and has no intention of being cared for in another household or being 'put away in an institution'. 'It would kill me if I had to go into a place like that' she exclaims. The fact that very many old people do go into places 'like that' for respite care and are none the worse for the experience is completely lost on her. Maddeningly, dependants refuse services much more often than do the carers whose needs might be greater. If you are in this latter sort of situation, strong advocacy is essential to ensure that your case as carer is properly put.

Financial help

Many carers are not particularly well off and if they have to abandon paid employment in order to care this can create excessive financial strain if the dependant cannot contribute sufficiently. As mentioned earlier, many extra expenses are generated by chronic illness or disablement necessitating extra help at home. You should secure up-to-date information on financial benefits. In the UK, and in other countries where similar benefits are available, entitlement depends upon three main factors;

1. *Age*: e.g. for pension, old age premium for income support, and income tax relief.

2. *Amount of money available as income and savings*: e.g. income support, housing benefit, and rebate for local taxes.

3. *Frailty and disability*: e.g. attendance allowance for the afflicted and the invalid care allowance payable to the carer.

It is essential that you receive expert advice to ensure that all the relevant benefits are claimed. If a care manager has not been assigned to your case, advice on these financial matters can be obtained from the local offices of the Department of Social Security, Age Concern, or the Citizen's Advice Bureau. The addresses and telephone numbers are listed in the business section of the local telephone directory.

Someone to talk to

The family doctor is normally the professional with the greatest power in relation to the elderly person's care and you must have ready access to him because his decisions affect many of the other service provisions. Also his advice and support can be invaluable both emotionally and practically. As already mentioned, he can give information about the patient's illnesses and disabilities and an explanation of what will be done to relieve the old person's suffering and what support you might be given. Since the doctor's time is somewhat limited, the community care organizer or some equivalent person from the health or social services organizations should be involved to let you talk through your problems at greater length and to devise solutions. The precise arrangements for organizing community care vary from place to place and change from time to time. The doctor should be able to point you in the right direction. For example, in our own locality, community care organizers are responsible for arranging a suitable 'care package' directly and in liaison with other carers such as district nurses. They can also arrange day care or a respite spell in residential care, subject to availability. They regularly review the care needs of the afflicted person.

However, even with the best will in the world, this may not be enough. You may require more than just a 'nuts and bolts' response to your troubles. You might want more opportunity to give vent to your feelings, about all the emotional and practical problems which beset you. Attendance at a relatives' support group can be helpful, especially in reducing the sense of social isolation you can feel if trapped in the caring role: 'I now know that I'm not the only one'. It also allows carers to share the practical know-how of caring and how to secure help. This knowledge can increase your assertiveness in the face of bureaucracy: 'Mrs Smith around the corner has that service to help with her Mum, why not me?' But there are snags to these groups if you have to attend regularly, because they eat into precious time, time which may have been bought by provision of a sitter or attendance of the dependant at day care. Also you may feel you would prefer to do other things in your time out. Some carers say 'It's not a real break, I want to get away from all that'. Carers of patients with certain diseases could benefit from belonging to a specialized local group, for example the Alzheimer's Disease Society or the Parkinson's Disease Society. These national societies provide information and support and also promote research in their special fields.

When the caring comes to an end, either by the death of your loved one or by her long-term admission to a residential home, hospital, or nursing home, you probably need time and some support until you adjust to the new situation. Many institutions encourage carers to continue to care in the new setting. Ask about this if you would like to continue to be actively involved, also ask if there is an 'in-house' relatives' support group. Although you have lost the burden of care, you have also lost a loved one or at least lost an intensely personal caring relationship which may virtually have consumed your life for years. Even if not bereaved, this can be a most traumatic time and you could feel engulfed by emotion and an overwhelming sense of fatigue. Soon you must turn your thoughts towards rebuilding the life you left in order to do the caring. While all this is going on you will still need lots of support from your family and friends. Be assured you did all that was expected of you, and more.

21 Death

Now that the developed nations have advanced so far towards the elimination of premature death (see Chapter 1), dying is increasingly something we do when we have become old. Once we are born, we have an excellent change of fulfilling our allotted three-score years and 15 or more, and so death has become in a sense the preserve of the old (Fig. 21.1). It is therefore perfectly legitimate

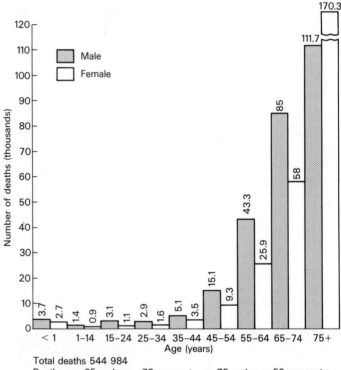

Total deaths 544 984
Deaths age 65 and over, 78 per cent, age 75 and over 52 per cent

Fig. 21.1 Age at death, England 1982.

Source: OPCS (1984). *Mortality statistics: area 1982*, Series DH5 No. 9. HMSO, London.

for ageing people to develop a degree of curiosity about the subject and there is nothing unwholesome about an objective examination of the most inevitable of all natural processes.

Children and teenagers are often surprised that their grandparents ever enjoy any respite from the contemplation of their impending death. But human psychology is remarkably adaptable and, although man is uniquely burdened by the knowledge of his own mortality, the burden does not seem to be unduly oppressive. There is some evidence that older people do become somewhat more preoccupied with death, though not overwhelmingly so, but also that they become readier to discuss the subject openly and often regard it with less dread than the young and middle-aged. This may be because life is less precious, or it may be because there is no longer a pressing need to complete a mass of unfinished business here on earth. As people age, a reasonably detached interest may develop. The dominating question may no longer be 'when?' Of greater moment perhaps is 'how?' and of more than passing interest may be 'where?'.

The fear of death has been divided into three main components: the regret at leaving the world, the anxiety that there is no afterlife but just nothingness, and the terror of the process of dying and its possible attendant suffering or indignity. The older we become, the less are we concerned with the first two of these, and it is really only the third that continues to be of major importance. Woody Allen's comment 'I'm not afraid to die, I just don't want to be there when it happens' is often quoted because it strikes such a precise chord with our own feelings and expresses unerringly a sentiment with which we can all identify.

When will I die?

The ageing process is not easy to define; but one of the few indisputable statements that can be made about it is that it represents an increase in our risk of dying within any given period of time (see Chapter 7). Even the developed nations have yet to eliminate congenital malformations, inborn diseases, and deliveries of very low birthweight babies, so the weeks and months following birth remain a relatively high-risk phase of life. Our chance of dying then plummets to a low-point which seems to occur around the age of 12, after which it starts to rise again. After the age of 30, our risk of death in any given day, month, or year doubles approximately every eight years.

We saw in Chapter 1 that life expectancy at birth has increased disproportionately during the past century by comparison with our residual years of expected life at later ages, but that life expectancies have nevertheless increased and are continuing to do so even in old age. Table 1.2 gave some figures and shows how many more years we can expect to live as we get older. Figure 21.1 demonstrates how vulnerable we become in our declining years. Some individual risk factors are given in Table 21.1.

Table 21.1   Factors affecting life expectancy.

Smoking	⎫	
Hypertension	⎬	Arterial disease risk factors
Hypercholesterolaemia		
Diabetes	⎭	
Sex	—	be a woman
Heredity	—	choose parents with care
Geography	—	Japanese live longest
Stature	—	being short is bad: if fat, being 'an apple' is worse than being 'a pear'
Origins	—	being a low birth-weight baby is bad
Palmistry	—	the line of life is actually on the ear lobe, where possession of a horizontal crease is adverse
Social class	—	life expectancy is better in the higher classes
Civil status	—	get married and stay that way!
Habits	—	diet, exercise, alcohol, activity

What are the main hazards?

Statistics are ways of looking at cohorts (groups) or populations and tell us little about individuals. After the childhood years accidents, violence, suicide, AIDS, and drug abuse become the main killers, although the numbers remain relatively small. Thereafter, broadly the same causes of death predominate throughout the age range (Fig. 21.2). Circulatory disorders are the great scourge of

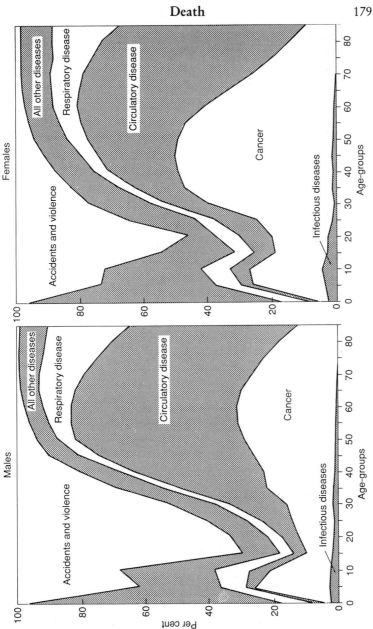

Fig. 21.2 Selected causes of death, by sex and age, in the UK 1980.
Source: Social Trends (1982), Chart 7.4.

men, and strokes and heart attacks take a greater toll of women than does cancer from about the age of 60 onwards. Pneumonia and other chest diseases make a fairly major impact in old age, and although not numerically enormous, the risk of accidental death rises surprisingly as we age, largely due to falls.

How do we die?

Although identifying the disease which causes death may tell us why death has occurred, it does not tell us how. The victim of coronary heart disease may die abruptly from cardiac arrest, or may sustain a series of myocardial infarcts which eventually cause so much replacement of heart muscle by fibrous tissue that the heart becomes a dilated, feebly contracting bag which over a period of months fails to keep the body supplied with oxygen which leads to progressive breathlessness and weakness.

Sudden death is probably what we would mostly choose for ourselves, although not all so-called high quality deaths are sudden and an abrupt exit from the world can be exceedingly shocking for our nearest and dearest. It is therefore fortunate that the common killing diseases can be so expeditious in their onslaught. Some of the more common high quality deaths are:

- cardiac arrest
- massive pulmonary embolism
- overwhelming bronchopneumonia
- accidental hypothermia
- diabetic crisis (ketoacidotic or hyperosmolar)
- overdose
- massive intracranial haemorrhage/cerebral infarction.

The certificate which doctors have to complete before a body can be cremated (to make sure that evidence of foul play is not destroyed) asks him to select one of four modes of death—exhaustion, coma, convulsions, or syncope. It is often very difficult to assign deaths into one of these four categories. A few people enter comatose states from which medical treatment fails to rescue them. Very large numbers of people suffering incurable disease lapse into a merciful state of clouded oblivion hours or sometimes days before they die. Few people these days die of epileptic convulsions. Considerable numbers might be regarded as dying in syncope, if the term is taken to embrace all forms of sudden death, that enviable exit defined by one professor of pathology as 'here one minute and gone the next'. Table 21.2 shows the likely causes

Table 21.2 Sudden death from natural causes.

Severe narrowing of coronary arteries
Cerebral haemorrhage
Pulmonary embolism
Inhalation of large pieces of food blocking larynx (especially in mentally
    ill or under influence of drugs/drink)
Dissecting aneurysms

of sudden death—in general they are occurrences of older age groups. Indeed, the event is uncommon under the age of 50, although cot death, asthma, epilepsy, and accidents do claim some young victims in a peremptory manner. It has been estimated that perhaps 10 per cent of people over the age of 50 die suddenly and unexpectedly: for the rest of us, a more protracted demise lies in store. Another estimate gives sudden unexpected death a 50 per cent share of the total, with prolonged terminal care 20 per cent, and the remainder being somewhere between the extremes.

Dying slowly

It is granted to relatively few of us to shuffle off this mortal coil in one of the highly enviable ways listed above. Cancer rates as the second leading cause of mortality in the UK after heart disease and claims one-fifth of deaths in Europe and North America. Cancer is often identified in the public mind with inevitable fatality, which is fallacious since a number of different diseases are included in the general category of cancer and many are curable. It is also identified with pain, particularly in the latter stages, and these two beliefs engender the fear that is so generally associated with 'the big C'. Various surveys have provided considerable ground for the latter fear, showing pain to be a prominent symptom in 58–84 per cent of patients with advanced cancer. Many of these surveys are based on hospice populations, which are far from typical, and some include comparatively trivial aches and pains, so the true figure for significant pain might be two out of three such patients. It has been concluded from various published reviews that some 25 per cent of all cancer patients die without relief from severe pain—a gloomy figure and an unnecessarily high one. Drugs such as morphine and its derivatives remain the sheet anchor of pain control and are effective in the large majority of cases if given sufficiently regularly in sufficient doses, although often, it has to be admitted, at an unacceptable cost in terms of clouding of consciousness, nausea, and constipation.

Pain is certainly not the only factor which can make dying a terrible experience, although it is perhaps the most feared and best documented. Others include fear, depression, institutionalization, dependency, confusion, indignity, immobility, nausea, breathlessness, lethargy, and constipation. These are all susceptible to amelioration in greatly varying degrees, but as has been mentioned, the final stage, whether of hours or a day or two, is commonly associated with a twilight state of gathering oblivion.

Where do we die?

Although almost all of us would express a wish to die in our own home, we are, ironically, over twice as likely in the event to die in hospital which seems to be widely regarded as the proper place to do it. In 1987, about 360 000 deaths in England and Wales, or 56 per cent of the total, took place in an NHS hospital and 135 000 at home. People in rural areas are more likely to die in their own homes than are city dwellers.

What is death?

This may seem to be a silly question because it is usually fairly obvious when someone is dead. This is particularly true in the case of someone expected to die. Death has traditionally been equated with cessation firstly of the heartbeat and then, very soon afterwards, of respiration. Prior to that, in a person who is known to have an unrecoverable illness, the state of clouded consciousness often lasts for a period of hours or days, during which time the respiratory effort may become progressively weaker. The introduction of cardiopulmonary resuscitation (CPR) in 1960 made it clear that survival was sometimes possible after cardiac arrest, and the requirement for 'beating-heart' organ donors necessitated a controversial new definition, that of brain-stem death.

The point is not that older people are likely to become potential beating-heart organ donors but that the definition of death is nothing like so clear-cut as it once was, and that dying is a process which has various stages, some of which are recoverable. Victims of hypothermia are especially liable to be thought dead. For these reasons, it is permissible to enquire whether there are some people who have first-hand information to impart as to what it is like to die, having effectively done it themselves.

Near-death experiences

Although most of those who have described their brushes with death have undergone serious illness or major surgery, not all of these uncomfortably close encounters have occurred against a high-technology background and a series published in 1892 involved mountaineers who had survived falls. Most recent reports have, however, emerged from hospital coronary care and intensive care units. The experiences of the survivors do tend to share certain features. Time becomes distorted and one's life is instantaneously seen in totality. A feeling of peace and joy is enhanced by images of a heavenly world full of mystical beings and deceased relatives, often reached by passing through a dark tunnel. 'Out of body' phenomena are common, in which the subject experiences dissociation from his physical self and may float in a position above the bed or operating table and from which he can look down upon his mortal remains and witness the frantic attempts of the hospital staff to resuscitate him. Whether these experiences do in fact tell us much about death is questionable and it may be that what they have in common is the psychological reaction to the perception of imminent death. It also has to be said that the features that they share are considerably fewer than the features that render each one unique, so that collections of such accounts are extremely readable whether or not one regards them as instructive.

What do they do with our bodies?

Any sudden and unexpected death will be reported to the coroner in England and so will deaths resulting from accidents or suicide or occurring in suspicious circumstances. Even where death has been undoubtedly due to natural causes, the doctor may notify the coroner if he is so unsure of the diagnosis that he feels unable to issue a death certificate. The coroner will usually order a post-mortem examination, but if he requires further clarification he may arrange for an inquest to be held. Around 32 per cent of all deaths are referred to the coroner and just under an eighth of these are the subject of an inquest. It is common practice, especially in teaching hospitals, for the medical team in charge of the case to request permission from the family of a deceased patient to carry out an autopsy even if the coroner has not been involved, as a great deal can be learned from coming face to face at last with the killer that has eluded detection or at least defeat. Permission is in fact both sought and granted in only 15 to 20 per cent of cases.

If you die in hospital or in a public place, your body is taken to the hospital mortuary and stored there for a day or two until the for-malities have been completed and the undertaker is permitted to take it away. Further disposal is then by burial or cremation, the latter having become increasingly popular and now accounting for 70 per cent of the 600 000 people who die each year in England and Wales.

Can my body be of use?

The most valuable act we can perform in this regard is to express a wish to donate our organs in the event of a catastrophe befalling us, and donor cards are generally available in doctors' surgeries and hospital clinics. It is widely assumed that the donor should be young and previously healthy, but this is not necessarily the case. The cornea can remain perfectly satisfactory well into old age. Kidneys are now accepted from donors up to the age of 70, provided there has not been a history of kidney disease or high blood pressure. It should be emphasized that there is always a shortage of donor organs and a queue of hopeful recipients.

The other way that our bodies can be of use to others when we have finished with them is by donating them to medical science. This in practice generally means that they are made available for dissection by medical students in a university department of anatomy. There are certain factors that render the body unsuitable for this purpose, such as removal of organs other than the eyes for corneal transplantation, the performance of a post-mortem exam-ination, amputation, cancer, tuberculosis, and AIDS. As long as the deceased person has provided written or witnessed oral evidence of their wish to donate their body for anatomical examination, anyone legally in possession of the body may authorize donation. It is advisable therefore to leave a written statement to this effect among your official papers if you wish to donate your body. It is then incumbent upon whoever is in possession of the body to notify the department of anatomy as soon as possible after death. The death is registered as quickly as possible and if it has occurred at home the body should be removed to a chapel of rest. The anatomy department will subsequently instruct a funeral director to arrange transfer of the body to the department. The body may be retained for up to three years, and individual parts occasionally for longer, but will eventually be released for burial or cremation, although the relatives or executors are not informed of this event.

In England it is not entirely clear who is, in fact, legally in possession of a body, since English law recognizes no ownership except in the case of individual organs or fluids removed and held for research purposes. In the case of deaths occurring in NHS hospitals the health authority is in possession of the body until it is claimed by a person with the right to possession—the coroner, executor, or next of kin. When someone dies at home, the house-holder is lawfully in possession.

Some research groups need extremely fresh material for the study of conditions such as Alzheimer's or Parkinson's disease. In order for this to be possible, it is clearly totally insufficient for instructions to be contained in a will and the matter must be discussed with the patient, if he has the capacity, and the relatives well before death. Again, witnessed oral instructions during the last illness are sufficient to enable action by the person in possession.

Can I afford to die?

Sadly, it has to be said that dying is an inflationary activity. The average cost of a burial in the UK rose by almost 25 per cent in 1990 to £920, while cremations rose 13 per cent to £712 (cremations are cheaper because there is no burial plot and no grave-diggers' charges). The cost of dying varies throughout the country, and is considerably more expensive if you die abroad. If you die on holiday in Spain, for example, it will cost £2500–£3000 to be flown home, so it is advisable to read that section of the small print in the travel insurance document. Age Concern operate a 'guaranteed funeral plan' by advance payment.

Voluntary euthanasia

A brief comment on this highly contentious topic is a fitting note on which to conclude this chapter. Euthanasia, in the sense of dying with dignity and without suffering, is a concept which would receive universal support, but the term is commonly misused to convey the deliberate termination of life using humane means, and in this sense it continues to stimulate intense public debate. It is easier to feel pity than to pass harsh moral judgement on elderly people who take their own lives for reasons of circumstance, depression, or physical sickness. We would seriously question whether they have the right to demand that their doctors should perform this service for them. It is a commonplace experience in the daily practice of geriatricians to encounter patients who are admitted to hospital as emergencies with distressing and grave diseases and who seriously request a lethal injection. 'What can you possibly do for me, doctor?' is a familiar lament. Many of these patients return to the out-patient clinic a few weeks later having happily resumed the tenor of their lives, delighted in the anticipation of several more years of active enjoyment. Even when the illness is an inevitably fatal one, it is generally possible to alleviate suffering.

It is also not uncommon for geriatricians to be less than heroic in their life-saving interventions when medical emergencies affect people with marked dementia, widespread cancer, or severe dependency. Philosophers often attack this stance and claim that this 'passive euthanasia' is in no way morally different from the administration of active euthanasia in the form of a deliberate lethal injection. This may or may not be so from the vantage point of an armchair, but such philosophical niceties are of little help to the clinician faced with the day-to-day decisions inseparable from the sharp end of medical practice.

22   Bereavement

There is a modern tendency to regard death and dying as essentially a medical and nursing problem, but this leaves an emotional void. Disregard for the spiritual, psychological, and social aspects of care may well increase the suffering of the supporting relatives and friends not only during the terminal illness but also after the death. In the UK, where religious beliefs are generally weak or non-existent, there is a lack of clear secular patterns of behaviour for these heart-rending situations. As a result people are often uncertain how to react. For example, should we encourage the newly bereaved to talk about the deceased and give vent to their feelings, or would that be too embarrassing?

Peace at the last for the dying, and humane and appropriate support for the bereaved are earnestly to be desired, but difficult to achieve if we have no obvious, socially acceptable models of behaviour to follow. A positive, constructive attitude is required because death is such an important part of each person's life. The purpose of this chapter is to explore the nature of human reaction to severe loss, especially the loss of a loved one, and to suggest ways in which ordinary people can be of help in this desperately unhappy situation. In late life especially, women are much more commonly bereaved than men and the wording here reflects this.

Reaction to loss

Bereavement is a reaction to loss, the loss of a loved one. The pain of grief is the price we pay for our love and commitment to another. Bereavement can be the most stressful major life event, surpassing marriage, the bringing-up of children, moving house, retirement, redundancy, a divorce, or losing an eye or a limb. Any severe loss can produce a bereavement type of reaction but none so profound as the loss of a loved one. All elderly people have some acquaintance with death through loss of parents and contemporaries, and adjustment to the prospect of the death of oneself or spouse will have taken place to a considerable extent. Even so, loss of spouse or of offspring can be exceedingly hard to bear. For some the bereavement reaction is a mixture of grief and relief, as for example, where the deceased was the victim of a long and distressing illness.

Loss of spouse is a complex loss of companion, audience, sexual partner, person to be cared for and thought about and who loved and cared for the bereaved person in a way that no one else did. All of this 'emotional nourishment' will have been provided for very many years during which the couple have shared innumerable experiences. To this extent the deceased is clearly irreplaceable. The deceased will have had many other roles in what might be referred to as the 'supply side' of the relationship; as gardener, cook, dog walker, home accountant, and so on. In many cases with the loss of the husband a sizeable tranche of pension income is also lost. Sudden, unexpected death is the most immediately distressful, but even when the loved one has been manifestly dying for months the final parting can be agonizing. Additionally there is a degree of stigma attached to widowhood in many Western societies. We may not insist on ritual suicide for widows but we do tend to pity and distance outselves from them.

Deprivation

In late life it is frequently the deprivational aspects of bereavement which are the hardest to bear. It is not simply the loss of love and 'emotional nourishment' but loss of the 'supply side' of the relationship as mentioned above. The deep sorrow over the love lost is immediate, but later, deprivation can be a major factor leading to loneliness and insecurity when grappling with life's problems. The widow must long for the support of her husband when faced with everyday tasks of a type that were formerly undertaken solely by him or by the couple in close co-operation, for example gardening, home decorating, or household repairs.

How the widow copes with the emotional loss and deprivation depends upon her personality, modified by the circumstances of the death and the situation in which she finds herself. Thus a clinging, dependent type of person left in a difficult social and financial situation is much less well placed than the sturdy, independent woman who is well-provided for financially and has a strong supporting social network. Generally speaking widows fare better than widowers. They are so much more familiar with all the tasks essential to survival and simply carry on doing these. Married men should familiarize themselves with basic life maintenance tasks in preparation for retirement and possible loss of partner. Although it is usually the man who dies first leaving a distraught widow to pick up the remains of her life, for a sizeable minority it will be the other way around.

Effects of bereavement on health

There is no doubt that the stresses of bereavement at any age can have adverse effects on health and cause an increase in mortality in the first year, more marked in widowers than in widows. For example a study in Sweden of widowed people showed a near 50 per cent increase in mortality among elderly widowers in the first three months of bereavement and some increase was observable years later. The increase in mortality in widows was less than half that in widowers. It has been suggested that the early excess mortality is directly due to emotional stress and the later deaths stem from lifestyle factors. The cause of these excess deaths is most often heart disease, but infections, accidents, suicides, and cirrhosis of the liver also play a part. Widowers who remarry survive better but whether the remarriage is protective or whether it is the biological élite who remarry is not known. It seems likely that self-neglect with poor diet, abuse of alcohol and tobacco, and possibly the adverse effects of prescribed medication such as tranquillizers, hypnotics, and antidepressants, are responsible for much of the delayed increase in morbidity and mortality.

The process of grief

Grief is not just an abnormal state of being which spontaneously fades away, although this is true to a certain extent. Grief is a process which has to be gone through. It is as if the suffering has to be tackled head on and there is much work '('grief work') to be done to make a full recovery. It takes time to work from the numbness precipitated by the initial shock through the emotional and social turmoil and despair, to a full recovery.

The components of grief

These include:

shock	disorganization	denial
depression	guilt	anxiety
anger	resolution	renewal.

Not every bereaved person goes through the same range of disturbances but there is much similarity. The process does not just affect the widow. The children will have their own grief to contend with while supporting and consoling the parent and in addition making practical arrangements for the registration of death, informing friends and relations, and organizing the funeral. There may be the deceased's belongings to collect from the hospital and important legal matters to attend to. Possibly there are items to be returned to public authorities like the NHS, social services, or the Red Cross, such as a special mattress, commode, or walking-frame. So many things require attention that some guidance (or a check-list) is usually needed. A useful booklet ('*What to do after a death: a guide to what you must do and the help you can get*') is available from the local social security department setting out the main actions required.

During the stage of initial shock, which can last for some days, the widow may appear to take everything in her stride. This can be misleading. 'Isn't it wonderful the way she's able to cope', people might say. Yet the severest pangs of grief often occur after the funeral, in the second week of bereavement when close family and friends have returned to their homes. When the full grief reaction reveals itself those left in support may begin to wonder if the bereaved is suffering a complete nervous breakdown and in need of specialist medical attention.

In the early days and weeks there may be loss of appetite, palpitations, headaches, muscular aches and pains, bouts of crying, much anxiety, and depression. Pangs of extreme grief come on from time to time precipitated by reminders of the deceased, for example waking at night alone in the double bed, sorting through his belongings, meeting a friend of his, and so on. There is great anxiety and restlessness, even panic at times, during the early weeks. It is not uncommon for the bereaved to search for the deceased yet this is known to be irrational. She may actually feel his presence, hear him speak, or see him at one of his usual tasks in the garden or sitting in his favourite chair. This behaviour and the hallucinations, which in other circumstances would be regarded as mental illness, are entirely normal in the context.

The early phase can be quite exhausting for everyone concerned, particularly when the bereaved expresses great anger or resentment towards those involved with the deceased such as the doctor, the clergyman, or God. She may be angry with herself as she struggles to make sense of it all: 'What went wrong? I should have insisted he saw the doctor earlier'; 'The doctor shouldn't have fobbed him off saying it is only "indigestion"'; 'What use has the priest been?'; 'If God is good how can he let people suffer so?'; 'Why was my husband so stupid about his health when he seemed so clever about most other things? He knew smoking was bad for the heart' and so on. Anger towards the husband adds to the guilt the bereaved may already feel because she believes that she did not do enough herself. Even supporting family and friends may come under attack. Anger, guilt, anxiety, and sadness combine to torment the bereaved. She desperately needs help, how best can this be given?

Helping the bereaved

We all need to understand the likely range of emotional disturbances and the associated practical problems. It is also crucial that we understand that the process of grief in its various phases must be worked through and that this is not a passive process. It is not simply a question of time being the great healer. The bereaved must be actively involved in the 'grief work' which is to be done. The bereaved need active emotional and practical support to work through their difficulties. On no account should expression of feelings be stifled; emotion should flood out. It must be understood that 'grief work' will be a painful business for the bereaved and all who attempt to help them.

In truth neither party can give the other what is most wanted. The widow would wish her husband alive and well, and so would her friends and relatives. The widow, realizing she cannot have her husband back, would at least wish to feel sufficiently well to cope on her own. Her supporters would earnestly desire this to be so but it will take time and much effort to achieve. Those who have themselves successfully worked their way through bereavement may be especially helpful to the newly bereaved.

Guidelines for helping the bereaved

Attention is drawn to some principles for bereavement counselling which provide valuable guidelines for ordinary people anxious to help.

1. *Admit the loss*

The widow must be allowed to 'actualize' the loss by encouraging conversation about the death and the fact that there can be no return from the dead.

2. *Identify and ventilate feelings*

Allow the bereaved sufficient 'emotional space' and the time for full and repeated expression of all the painful feelings which torment her. As Shakespeare wrote:

> 'Give sorrow words: the grief that does not speak
> Whispers the o'er-fraught heart, and bids it break'.

3. *Explore life without the deceased*

There may be practical problems to solve but major long-term decisions such as moving in with a relative or giving up a part-time job should be postponed. A move of residence is almost always best postponed for at least a year although a temporary stay or a series of stays with a caring relative or friend is often sensible in the early weeks or months.

4. *Discourage emotional withdrawal*

Social activity away from the home is to be encouraged. There is a need to make or renew friendships; 'not to replace Dad but to fill the gap'. It is best to avoid deep or emotional relationships at this time; the bereaved person needs to be on an even keel emotionally before that happens.

5. *Allow time for grief*

Grief work takes both time and trouble, and there are no short cuts. No benefit comes from superficial words of solace or reassurances such as 'don't worry, time is a great healer' or 'you'll soon get over it'. Positive, painful effort is required to complete the grieving process if full restoration is to occur.

6. *Interpret normal behaviour*

People should understand the reasons for the bizarre mental state, physical actions, and extraordinary feelings of the widow and patiently reassure her that she is not 'going mad'.

7. Allow for individual differences

Each person is unique and bereavement reactions reflect this individuality. The relatives and friends must avoid imposing personal judgements as to how things ought to be going. 'You should be over all this by now, Mum', is likely to reinforce the widow's belief that she has gone crazy.

8. Provide continuing support

Intermittent but continuing support may be required for a year or more, and possibly indefinitely, from the close family. However 'unsupported' spells are necessary to allow personal readjustments to be made. Support is needed especially at critical times such as Christmas, family birthdays, the wedding anniversary, and notably around the anniversary of the death.

9. Consider the coping style

For example, recourse to alcohol or reliance on sedatives is not a good way to cope. It is always a mistake to try to blot out the anguish with these substances. Their use can impede the grieving process and may lead to ill health.

10. Seek medical help when things appear to be going wrong

The main indications for specialist help are when the acute phase appears unduly prolonged, when the coping style is abnormal, or physical illness supervenes or is exacerbated. The doctor can call on other agencies as required, for example specialist bereavement counselling from the local branch of CRUSE, a national organization providing help and support to the bereaved of all ages. The local branch may also offer social activities designed especially for those who find it difficult to go out and meet people in the absence of their loved one. Practical advice can also be obtained from the local branch of organizations like Age Concern and from the Citizens' Advice Bureau.

Further reading

Bond, J. and Coleman, P., (1990) *Ageing in society*. Sage, London.

Centre for policy on ageing (1989). *World directory of old age*. Longman, Harlow.

Comfort, A. (1979). *The biology of senescence* (3rd edition). Churchill Livingstone, Edinburgh.

Hughes, M. (ed.) (1989). *Bodyclock*. Weidenfeld and Nicolson, London.

Jefferys, M. (ed.) (1989). Growing old in the twentieth century, Routledge, London.

Joshi, H. (ed.) (1989). The changing population of Britain. Blackwell, Oxford.

Kenney, R. A. (1989). *Physiology of ageing*, (2nd edition). Year Book Medical Publishers, Chicago.

Laslett, P. (1989). *A fresh map of life*. Weidenfield, London.

Ludwig, F. C. (ed.) (1991). *Life span extension*. Springer, New York.

Mandelstam, D. (1989). *Understanding incontinence*. Chapman and Hall, London.

Parkes, C. M. (1986). *Bereavement: studies in grief in adult life* (2nd edition). Tavistock, London.

Publications by Age Concern, England:

Your rights (1990–91).

Life in the sun by Nancy Tuft.

In control—help with incontinence by Penny Mares.

Housing options for older people by David Bookbinder.

Using your home as capital by Cecil Hinton.

The foot care book by Judith Kemp.

At home in a home by Pat young.

Living, loving, and ageing by Wendy and Sally Greengross.

Trimmer, E. J. (1967). *Rejuvenation: the history of an idea*. Robert Hale, London.

Warner, A. M. (ed.) (1989). *Human ageing and later life*. Edward Arnold, London.

Wells, N. and Freer, C. (eds) (1989). *The ageing population*. MacMillan, Basingstoke.

Wilson, I. (1987). *The after death experience*. Sidgwick and Jackson, London.

Worden, J. W. (1983). *Grief counselling and grief therapy*. Tavistock, London.

Appendix A: Glossary

AIDS. Acquired immune deficiency syndrome. Caused by a virus (HIV) transmitted in the blood and other body fluids. Often fatal because of severe loss of resistance to infection and cancer. See HIV.

Alzheimer's disease. A serious disorder of the brain causing progressive dementia. This form of dementia (q.v.) affects many old people. Alois Alzheimer, German neurologist, d. 1915.

Amines. A group of chemical compounds formed from ammonia by combining with an organic radical or radicals, and often active in transmitting nerve impulses. See neurotransmitter.

Amyloid. An abnormal, complex, starch-like material which accumulates in various tissues with ageing; also produced excessively in certain disease states.

Aneuploidy. An unbalanced set of chromosomes, with deviation from the usual paired arrangement. There may be too many chromosomes, as in Down's syndrome where there is an extra chromosome number 21, or too few. Individuals exhibiting aneuploidy are usually physically abnormal in some way.

Angina. Full name angina pectoris. Attack of chest pain due to inadequate blood supply to the heart. The pain is of variable intensity and with a sense of constriction or suffocation; usually brought on by exertion, emotion, or exposure to cold, and of short duration.

Atherosclerosis (Atheroma, Arteriosclerosis). Degenerative disease in which the arteries are narrowed by patchy deposition of fatty substances, such as cholesterol, in the lining of the vessel.

Autoimmunity. A condition caused by immune responses against the body's own tissues; implicated in a wide range of disorders such as pernicious anaemia, thyroid failure, and rheumatoid arthritis. See also immune system.

Cerebral. Of, or pertaining to, the cerebrum, the higher part of the brain which integrates complex functions. Also used to indicate intellectual, as opposed to emotional, behaviour.

Cholecystogram. X-ray of the gallbladder using a contrast medium, especially to detect gallstones. Now largely replaced by the ultrasound scan.

Cholesterol. A steroid alcohol, manufactured in the liver and present normally in many tissues of the body and in animal fats in the diet. Present in excess in atheroma, gallstones, and some other diseases.

Chromosomes. Threads of DNA (q.v.) which carry genetic information. Normally there are 23 pairs of chromosomes in the nucleus of each cell. See also gene.

Collagen. The main supporting protein in the connective tissues of the body.

Cornea. The transparent, circular, front part of the eyeball.

Coronary arteries. The arteries supplying blood to the heart muscle or myocardium. See also myocardial infarction.

Cytoplasm. The living substance of the cell, excluding the nucleus, and surrounded by the cell wall.

Dementia. A chronic, progressive disease of the brain with loss of memory and intellect, associated with emotional disturbance and mental confusion; affects one in five of those aged 80 years and over in UK. As the disease progresses, behaviour out of keeping with the previous personality, restlessness, especially nocturnal, and incontinence of urine, and later of faeces, occur.

Demography. Study of statistics relating to births, deaths, and diseases so as to characterize and predict changes in a given population.

Diabetes. Full name diabetes mellitus. A disease in which the level of glucose (a sugar) in the blood is too high and so has to be excreted in large amounts in the urine.

Diuretic. A drug used to increase the production of urine and so disperse fluid (water and salts) in conditions such as heart failure.

DNA. Deoxyribonucleic acid. The carrier of genetic information; the molecule has a double helix configuration and each chain has information completely specifying the other chain.

Electroencephalogram (EEG). A record of the brain's activity traced by an electroencephalograph; often shows abnormalities in epilepsy.

Enzyme. A protein which speeds up a specific biochemical reaction.

Fibroblasts. Fibre-producing cells of connecting tissue forming the fibrous, supporting, and binding tissues throughout the body.

Gene. The basic unit of heredity, carried in a specific location on each of a pair of chromosomes (q.v.). Each pair of genes controls a particular inherited characteristic of the individual.

General Practitioner (GP). A doctor who, usually in partnership with others, plans and provides comprehensive primary health care for people of any age or sex, on a continuing basis (US: Family Physician.)

Glomerulus. The cluster of small blood vessels (capillaries) protruding into the expanded first part of the tubule of the nephron (q.v.).

Hernia. Protrusion of intestine or other tissue through some abnormal opening, especially through the wall of the abdomen (abdominal hernia), commonly called a rupture.

Hiatus hernia. A common condition, seldom serious, in which part of the stomach extends above the diaphragm into the chest. May allow stomach acid to flow into the oesophagus (gullet), causing indigestion, bleeding, or even narrowing (stricture) of the oesophagus.

HIV. Human immunodeficiency virus. See AIDS.

Homeostasis. The ability to maintain a constant internal physical and chemical environment despite variations in the external environment.

Hormone replacement therapy (HRT). Treatment of hormone deficiency, especially use of the female sex hormones in the postmenopause.

Immune system. The body's mechanisms, chemical and cellular, for recognizing and responding specifically to a wide range of 'foreign' (i.e. not normally present in the body) substances, which come from microbes, plants, and animals. Immune responses protect against infection but can cause unwanted disease as well as rejection of transplanted tissues. See also autoimmune.

Infarction. Death of an organ, or part of an organ, due to interruption of its blood supply. Infarct—the area of tissue so affected, or the clinical occurrence.

Involution. The reduction in size and function of an organ in old age or when its purpose has been fulfilled, for example involution of the ovaries at the menopause.

Ischaemia. Deficiency of blood supply to a part of the body.

Lean body mass. The fat-free mass of the body; excludes the metabolically inactive storage fat.

Leukaemia. Malignant disease (cancer) of white blood cells; classified on the basis of cell type and speed of onset.

Life expectancy. The likely age at which death will occur, taking into account premature death due to disease and accidents. Currently, for the newborn in developed countries, it is between 70 and 80 years.

Lifespan. The genetically determined length of life of the species; for humankind (the longest-lived mammalian species) probably a maximum of 110–120 years.

Lipofuscin. Pigmented granules which develop with ageing inside cells in many tissues, especially the brain, muscle, liver and kidney.

Mechanoreceptor. A specialized nerve ending, sensitive to mechanical pressure or distortion, providing input to the nervous system on movement, touch, and sound.

Melanin. The dark brown or black pigment found especially in the skin and iris of the eye; its increased production in the skin on exposure to sunlight causes tanning.

Melanoma. A malignant tumour of the melanin-producing cells.

Metabolism. Chemical processes by which energy is made available and the substance of the body is built up and maintained. Catabolism is the process of breaking down complex substances into simple ones, and anaoblism is the process whereby complex molecules, for example, proteins, are synthesized from nutrients.

Micturition. The act of passing urine; urination.

Morbidity. The condition of being diseased. Morbidity rate refers to the ratio of sick to well persons in the community.

Mucin. A glycoprotein; the chief constituent of mucus, a natural, slimy substance which lubricates and protects delicate membranes lining cavities, for example in the lungs, mouth, gut, and vagina.

Myocardial infarction. Death of part of the heart muscle (myocardium) due to inadequate blood flow through the coronary arteries, which supply only the heart.

Myxoedema. A condition due to inadequate function of the thyroid gland. There is a general slowing of mental and physical activity together with deposition of mucin (q.v.) in the skin and other tissues.

Nephron. The structural and functional unit of the kidney, consisting of a glomerulus (q.v.), which filters the blood, and a long, complex tubule which alters the filtrate, by processes of selective secretion and reabsorption of water and chemicals, to produce urine. Each kidney has about a million nephrons and they are the main means by which the volume and constituents of the body fluids are kept within the normal range.

Neurone. A nerve cell and its appendages.

Neurotransmitter. A chemical substance, usually an amine, released by a neurone (q.v.), and which transmits an impulse to another neurone, a gland cell, or a muscle fibre.

Nucleolus. (pl. nucleoli). A small, dense, spherical structure found within the cell nucleus.

Oedema. Accumulation of excess fluid (salt and water) in the tissues.

Osteomalacia. A painful condition in which the bones are softened and low in calcium content and the muscles are weak; due especially to lack of exposure to sunlight, dietetic deficiency of vitamin D and calcium, or impaired absorption.

Osteoporosis. Diminution of bone mass leading to increased risk of fracture, especially affecting the spine and limbs; associated particularly with ageing and the menopause.

Paget's disease. A disease of bone characterized by distortion of the bony architecture both internal and external. Usually innocuous but if severe can cause many problems including pain, deformity, fracture, and pressure on important structures. Sir James Paget, English surgeon, d. 1899.

Palliative. A treatment to alleviate a disease without curing it; includes surgical procedures. Palliation.

Paraphrenia. A form of paranoid schizophrenia seen especially in later life.

Parkinson's disease. A progressive disorder of muscular control due to loss of the neurotransmitter (q.v.) dopamine in the brain; characterized by slowness of movement, tremor, and muscular rigidity. Parkinsonism refers to these symptoms and signs. Sir James Parkinson, English surgeon, d. 1824.

Pathological. Caused by physical or mental disorder. For example a pathological fracture is one due to disease of the bone rather than due solely to trauma.

Prosthesis. An artificial part supplied to remedy a deficiency; examples include false teeth, artificial limbs, plastic lens implants, and artificial heart valves.

Rectangularization. A term coined to describe the progressive change in appearance of graphs plotting human survival made at intervals over the centuries. These graphs, called survival curves, have become 'rectangularized' because populations in the developed countries have such low age-specific death rates at all ages, until extreme old age. See text.

RNA. Transmits information from DNA (q.v.) to the protein-forming systems of the cell (including enzymes, q.v.).

Senescence. The process or condition of growing old, especially the accumulation of deleterious ageing processes.

Syncope. A temporary loss of consciousness due to sudden failure of blood supply to the brain.

Therapeutic. Contributing to the treatment of disease.

Third age. The age at which people are able to leave work and follow other interests—a golden age. Unlike Shakespeare the authors are thinking in terms of four 'ages' of man! The first age being that of growth and development, the second of earning a living and raising a family, and unless sudden death occurs, the fourth is likely to be one of terminal decline, decrepitude, and pre-death dependency.

Thrombosis. The coagulation of blood in a blood vessel. May obstruct the blood flow in that vessel or detach and obstruct other vessels (embolization).

Thyroid. A gland in the neck which produces the hormone thyroxine to regulate metabolism. Overactivity of the gland is called hyperthyroidism or thyrotoxicosis; underactivity of the gland, hypothyroidism or myxoedema (q.v.).

Tumour. A swelling, especially an abnormal growth of tissue; not necessarily a cancer.

Appendix B: Useful addresses

United Kingdom

Note that many of these organizations have local branches; See business section of local telephone directory.

Age Concern
1268 London Road
London SW16 4EJ
081 679 8000
(contact local organizations)

Alzheimer Disease Society
158–160 Balham High Road
London SW12 9BN
081 675 6557
(and local branches)

Arthritis Care
6 Grosvenor Crescent
London SW1X 7ER
071 235 0902

British Epilepsy Association
Ansley House
40 Hanover Square
Leeds LS3 1BE
0532 439393

British Geriatrics Society
1 St Andrew's Place
Regent's Park
London NW1 4LB
071 935 4004

British Nursing Association
470 Oxford Street
London W1N 0HQ
071 629 9030
(nursing agency)

Carers National Association
29 Chilworth Mews
London W2 3RG
071 724 776

Centre for Policy on Ageing
25–31 Ironmonger Row
London EC1V 3QP
071 253 1787

Chest, Heart and Stroke
Association
Tavistock House North
Tavistock Square
London WC1H 9SE
071 387 3012
(contact local stroke club)

Citizens' Advice Bureau
Middleton House
115–123 Pentonville Road
London N1 9LZ
071 833 2181

Counsel and Care for the Elderly
Twyman House
16 Bonny Street
London NW1 9PG
071 485 1550

Court of Protection
(apply to Chief Clerk)
25 Store Street
London WC1E 7BP
071 636 6877

CRUSE
Cruse House
126 Sheen Road
Richmond
Surrey TW9 1UR
081 940 4818
(counselling and advice to the
widowed)

The Disabled Living Foundation
380–384 Harrow Road
London W9 2HV
071 289 6111

Health Education Authority
Hamilton House
Mabledon Place
London WC1H 9TX
071 631 0930

Help the Aged
St James' Walk
London EC1R 0BE
071 253 0253

Marie Curie Memorial Foundation
28 Belgrave Square
London SW1
071 235 3325

National Care Homes Association
5 Bloomsbury Place
London WC1
071 436 1871

Office of Population Censuses and
Surveys (OPCS)
St Catherine's House
10 Kingsway
London WC2

Parkinson's Disease Society
36 Portland Place
London W1N 3DE
071 323 1174

Pre-Retirement Association
19 Undine Street
London SW17
081 767 3225

Registered Nursing Home
Association
75 Portland Place
London W1N 4AA
071 631 1524

Research into Ageing
49 Queen Victoria Street
London EC4 4SA
071 236 4365

The Royal National Institute for
the Blind
224 Great Portland Street
London W1N 6AA
071 788 1266

The Royal National Institute for
the Deaf
105 Gower Street
London WC1E 6AH
071 387 8079

Samaritans
46 Marshall Street
London W1
071 439 2224

Social Trends
A useful review of official statistical
information. Obtainable from
booksellers, Government
Bookshops (e.g. 49 High Holborn,
London, WC1V 6HB) and Open
University Educational Enterprises
Ltd, 12 Cofferidge Close, Stony
Stratford, Milton Keynes, MK11
1BY (Tel: 0908 566744)

The University of the Third Age
6 Parkside Gardens
London SW19 5EY
081 947 0401

The Voluntary Euthanasia Society
13 Prince of Wales Terrace
London W8 5PG
071 937 7770

United States

American Association of Retired
Persons (includes Worker Equity
Department) 601 E Street, NW
Washington DC 20049 USA
(Much useful information)

Gray Panthers
3700 Chestnut Street
Philadelphia PA 19104
(Militant anti-ageism)

Index

abuse of elderly 170
accommodation 31
acidity 117
adaptations 46
  to home 38
age, third 9
Age Concern 173, 200
  as a weapon 13
ageing, attempts to control 59–62
  biology 48 *et seq.*
  normal 54–9
ages of man 8
aids 46
aids and appliances 40
alcohol 81
allowance, attendance 40
alcohol 81
allowance, attendance 39
  invalid care 39
altered bowel habit 122
Alzheimer's disease 49, 84 *et seq.*
Alzheimer's Disease Society 174, 200
amyloid 49
aneuploidy 49
aneurysm, aorta 132
angina 131
annual review 41
antidepressants 83
anxiety 84
appetite loss 115
appliances 40
arteriosclerosis 129–32
arthritis 97–8
  hips 38
arthritis and rheumatism 168
atheroma 129–32
atherosclerosis 90, 91, 129–32
attendance allowance 39
audiogram 140
autonomic nervous system 68
autopsy 184

balance 57
baldness 146
barium meal 117

'benign senescent forgetfulness' 86
bereavement 187–93
  effects on health 180
  how to help 191–3
'biological clock' 49
birth rates 6
bladder 124 *et seq.*
blindness 136, 168
blood flow, cerebral 71
blood pressure 132
body composition 55, 63 *et seq.*
body, disposal of 184
  donation 184
  organ donation 184
bone density 108
brain, 71 *et seq.*
  ageing 55–6
breathlessness 98
burial 185

calluses 146
campylobacter 114
cancer 148–57
  in bones 108
  causes 152–4
  diagnosis 148–9
  incidence 150–2
  manifestations 149
  prevention 156–7
  treatment 155–6
capacity, testamentary 87
cardiac failure 133–4
care, manager 171
  package 171, 174
care homes 32
carers 14, 168
  stress on 169–71
  support for 170–5
  support groups 174
caring, for infirm elderly at home
    167–75
cataract 138
catheter 128
cells, ageing of 49

cerebral blood flow 71
  cortex 71
  haemorrhage 90–1
  infarction 90–1
childhood mortality 7
chiropody 43, 146
chiropodists 147
chromosomes 49
chromosome 21, 49, 86
circulation 57
Citizens Advice Bureau 173, 193, 200
claudication, intermittent 131
'clock, biological' 49
cold, exposure 69
colonic cancer 123
community care assistants 45
community care organizer 174
community care services 166, 172–5
community nurses 42
community services 41
composition, of body 63 *et seq.*
confusion 89
connective tissue, ageing 51
constipation 118, 122
continuing care communities 33
coroner 184
cortex, cerebral 71
Court of Protection 88
cremation 185
Crohn's disease 121
cross-linkage 51
CRUSE 193, 201
crystallins 51
cystitis 127

deafness 139–40, 168
death 176 *et seq.*
  causes 178–80
  place 182
  sudden 180–1
dehydration 64, 65
delirium 89
dementia 84 *et seq.*, 168
demography 1
dental services 43
dental treatment 143
dentures 143
deoxyribonucleic acid (DNA) 50
Department of Geriatric Medicine 43
depression 82–4
deprivation, in bereavement 188–9
diabetes 67
diarrhoea 120, 122

diet 112
diet, diabetic 67
dietary fibre 122, 118
Diogenes syndrome 80–1
Diploma in Geriatric Medicine 25
disability 5 *et seq.*, 168
disulphide bonds 51
diverticular disease 120–21
dizziness 98
Down's syndrome 49, 86
driving 109
drugs, use by elderly 161–2
  adverse effects 160–1, 165–6
  response in elderly people 165–6
duodenum 116–17

eczema 145
electroconvulsive therapy 83
endoscopy 116
environmental hazards 102
euthanasia 186
exercise, effects of 55, 60
expectation, life 5
eye tests 139

facial hair 146
faintness 98
falls 100, 102, 103
  dangers 102
family doctor 25, 41, 173–4
family ties 29
fertility, loss of 58
fibroblasts, divisions 49
finance in retirement 27
fitness 23, 60
fluid accumulation 66
flying, hazards 66, 111
food safety 114
foot care assistant 147
fractures 103
frame, walking or Zimmer 39
free oxygen radicals 50
function, changes in 55
  declining 53
funeral 185

gait 54
gallbladder 116
gallstones 118
gangrene 131
gastroscopy 117
general practitioner 25, 41
Gerovital 62
ginseng 61

glaucoma 137
gout 100
grief, component 189
  process 189–9

handicap 5
Hayflick 49
health in retirement 24
health visitors 42
hearing 56–7
hearing aids 141
heart 57, 129 *et seq.*
  disease 168
  failure 133–4
heartburn 116, 117
help, with domestic tasks 167
  for bereaved 191–3
  for carers 170
  financial 173
  with personal care 167
hiatus hernia 116, 117
hip fractures 103, 104
home helps 45
homeostasis, failure of 51, 64
hormone replacement therapy (HRT)
  61, 107
housebound 5
household structure 34
HRT 61
hypotension, orthostatic or postural 68
hypothermia 69

illness, long term 158
  care for at home 167–75
immunity, and ageing 51
impairment 5
incontinence 124 *et seq.* 168
  faecal 121
indigestion 117
infarction, cerebral 90–1
  myocardial 131
infirm elderly, caring for 167–75
inflammatory bowel disease 121
influenza vaccination 135
insomnia 77–8
institutional neurosis 84
intelligence testing 73–6
intertrigo 145
intermittent claudication 131
invalid care allowance 39
itching 144

jaundice 118

keyhole surgery 118
key worker 171
kidneys 58, 64

laxatives 113, 120
lean body mass 63
legs, restless 79
leg ulcers 145
libido 58
life expectancy 5
  factors affecting 178
  how to improve it 60
life span 7
lipofuscin 49, 71
listeria 114
living with relatives 34
local authority services 45
longevity 8
  animals 52
lunch clubs 46
lungs 57–8, 135

meals-on-wheels 46
medicines 158–66
  boxes 163
  chart 163
  development of 159–61
  response in elderly people 165
  taking as doctor ordered 162–5
memory 75
menopause 58, 61, 107
mental depression 168
Mental Health Act 89
metabolism, ageing 55
mobility 97
  allowance 111
  reduced 37, 39
mobilization 158–66
  display chart 163
moles 144
mortality, childhood 7
motor neurone disease 95, 97
mutations 50
myocardial infarction 131
myxoedema 120

National Assistance Act, section 47, 89
National Health Service 41
nausea 116
near-death experiences 183
nephrons 57
nerves, peripheral 72
nervous system 72

ageing 55
autonomic 68
central 72
neurofibrillary tangles 86
neurons, loss of 71, 86
neurosis, institutional 84
neurotransmitters 56, 71, 86
non-steroidal anti-inflammatory drugs
(NSAIDS) 160–1

occupational therapist 171
oesophagus 116
oestrogen 107
Office of Population Censuses and
Surveys 97
opticians 43
orgasm 59
osteomalacia 108
osteoporosis 106
otosclerosis 141
oxygen, lack 58

pacemaker, cardiac 134
paranoid psychosis 82
paraphrenia 82
Parkinson's disease 85, 94–5
Parkinson's Disease Society 174, 201
pensions 28
peptic ulcer 117
personal alarm 32, 45
personality 76
pharmaceutical companies 159–60
physiotherapist 42, 172
piles 123
plaques, senile 71, 86
pneumonia 135
population, projected 4, 10
post-mortem examination 184
posture 54, 57
presbycusis 139
prescriptions, NHS 159
primary care team 41
private health insurance 44
progesterone 107
prostrate 125
protein, defective 50
psychiatry, of old age 80 *et seq.*
psychology, of ageing 73–7

reaction times 74
reaction to loss 187–91
Red Cross 190
rejuvenation, attempt at 60

reminiscence 15
respite care 172–3
restless legs 79
retina 138
retirement 19
timing 20
rheumatoid arthritis 99
ribonucleic acid (RNA) 50
ribosomes 50
risks 13
road accidents 109
routine, in retirement 25

salmonella 114
Samaritans 170, 201
self-neglect 80
senescence 1
senile plaques 71, 86
senile squalor 80
sex 58–9
sexual activity 58
sexual responsiveness 59
sheltered housing 32
shingles 145
skin 144
sleep 77
snoring 78
speech defects 39
spring-lift chair 38
squalor, senile 80
stance 54
state pension 44
stomach 116, 117
stroke 90–4, 97, 168
clubs 39
suicide 83
'superoxide' radicals 50
survival curves 2, 3
rectangularization 3
swelling, feet/ankles 66

tangles, neurofibrillary 86
teeth 142
testamentary capacity 7
third age 9, 19
thirst 65
thrombosis, venous 66
thymus 51
tinnitus 142
tiredness 98
toenails 146
transient ischaemic attacks 131
transport 46, 109

treatment
  medical 159
  surgical 159
trips 107
tumours
  benign 148
  malignant 148
turns 102

urine, incontinence 124 *et seq.*
  production of 64

vaginitis, atrophic 126
venous thrombosis 66
vision 56
vitamins 112–113
  vitamin D 108

vitamin E
volunteer 13
vomiting 116

walking 54
walking frame 39
walking stick 39
wardens 45
warts 144
wax, in ears 140
weight loss 115
wheelchair 37
woopies 27
wrist fractures 103, 105
WRVS 46

Zimmer frame 39